Democratic Science Teaching

CULTURAL PERSPECTIVES IN SCIENCE EDUCATION:
RESEARCH DIALOGS

Volume 3

Series editor
Kenneth Tobin, *The Graduate Center, City University of New York, USA*
Catherine Milne, *Steinhardt School o Culture, Education, and Human Development, New York University*

Scope
Research dialogs consists of books written for undergraduate and graduate students of science education, teachers, parents, policy makers, and the public at large. Research dialogs bridge theory, research, and the practice of science education. Books in the series focus on what we know about key topics in science education – including, teaching, connecting the learning of science to the culture of students, emotions and the learning of science, labs, field trips, involving parents, science and everyday life, scientific literacy, including the latest technologies to facilitate science learning, expanding the roles of students, after school programs, museums and science, doing dissections, etc.

Democratic Science Teaching

Building the Expertise to Empower Low-Income
Minority Youth in Science

Edited by

Sreyashi Jhumki Basu
New York University, USA

Angela Calabrese Barton
Michigan State University, USA

Edna Tan
University of North Carolina at Greensboro, USA

SENSE PUBLISHERS
ROTTERDAM/BOSTON/TAIPEI

A C.I.P. record for this book is available from the Library of Congress.

ISBN: 978-94-6091-368-6 (paperback)
ISBN: 978-94-6091-369-3 (hardback)
ISBN: 978-94-6091-370-9 (e-book)

Published by: Sense Publishers,
P.O. Box 21858,
3001 AW Rotterdam,
The Netherlands
www.sensepublishers.com

Printed on acid-free paper

TABLE OF CONTENTS

ANGELA CALABRESE BARTON, JHUMKI BASU,
VERNEDA JOHNSON AND EDNA TAN (ALPHABETICAL)

1. INTRODUCTION

JHUMKI'S JOURNAL ENTRY

Each day I would walk into my class at a public school in a Caribbean neighborhood in Brooklyn, I would believe that my students could and would become leading scientists of their generation and smart, articulate citizens able to shape the directions in which science led their world; young people who would use science to make change in the world.

And yet, time and again, I noted reality. Amidst a discussion of radioactivity, a knock-down fight broke out in my classroom between two intelligent, confident girls. A previously-incarcerated student who had spent hours after-school powering motors with solar panels was arrested for assault, moments before he was to proudly present his findings at the annual science fair. This recidivism occurred despite hours of individualized support from his teachers and father. He spent time in prison rather than preparing for his dream career in mechanical engineering. A medicine and engineering course I taught evolved into a time for "literacy-building," undermined by a national emphasis on reading and math. A student deeply engaged with robotics had to "choose" between a science course and his special education services.

Meanwhile, engagement and excellence in my class were episodic. Every student boldly presented "original" work at the annual science fair and developed series and parallel circuits for powering household objects. But I'm quite sure that many students could not imagine how uncertainties about dark energy were relevant to their lives. Homework was likely often not completed because it did not have ties to the substance of students' lives. As a teacher, I probably often assumed that what mattered to me mattered to all my students, that the joys and rewards of learning science were obvious, rather than situated in paradigms that excluded the backgrounds, aspirations and Discourse of many of my students.

These realities are not all realities. My students in Brooklyn cared about academic success. Ask almost any student, and she will tell you that she wants to improve her grades, be on honor roll, pursue a successful career. Ask most parents, and they will want these same things for their children. It seems the issues are more of resources and paradigms. The girls at the elite private school where I taught for two years often came from extremely wealthy families with a history of social and financial success and high-quality private elementary- and middle-school educations. They attended a resource-rich school offering the most challenging classes and

S.J. Basu et al., (eds.), Democratic Science Teaching: Building the Expertise to Empower Low-Income Minority Youth in Science, 1–20.

were told time and again by peers, teachers, families and the world that they had achieved plenty and could be anything they dreamed to be.

Where in their academic life, particularly in science, were the life histories of my students in Brooklyn valued? Were any connections built between how science is traditionally taught and the farm on which one of my students grew up? Clearly not – she said this had nothing to do with science. Did one young man's delight in building toy boats as a child emerge through opportunities in his science classes? Did the young man engrossed with solar panels demonstrate his leadership skill in his science class? Did the 8th grader who tapped his pencil and squirmed endlessly in science class ever get time and space to exhibit his aptitude for building? And were these students told over and over, in what was formally said and offered to them, that they had the potential to learn science and be young scientists? Or instead, were they simply told to either adapt to the way science was taught or give up on their love of inquiry and knowledge?

RE/FRAMING URBAN SCIENCE EDUCATION IN A DEMOCRATIC SOCIETY

The seminal report, A Nation at Risk (1983) (ANAR), laid out the scenario that public schools would face in the coming decades, if significant changes were not made to the public education systems in place. Many of our schools located in growing urban centers were in crisis. Operating in deteriorating buildings, staffed by under prepared and unlicensed teachers, working in under resourced classrooms, not to mention the trend to staff inner city schools, that traditionally serve the academically neediest students, with the newest least prepared teachers. More egregious was the dysfunction in urban schools, the resulting student failure, and the reproduction of a 'culture of failure' within schools and communities. ANAR was published almost twenty years ago. Since that time many studies, narratives, and reports have commented on the factors that most impact upon urban school success and urban student achievement. Additionally, there is no shortage of information on what is 'wrong' in urban centers, including their schools.

Almost 20% of the nation's students are living in poverty, with numbers increasing under the recession that begun in 2008. But in large urban centers, like New York City, Atlanta, Houston and Los Angeles, that number more than doubles to 35–45% (Institute for Research on Poverty, 2010). Further, nearly 40% of urban students are attending high poverty schools. Students living in poverty are more likely to attend schools with outdated texts, are offered fewer opportunities to participate in summer or enrichment programs, have less access to certified teachers in math and science, and consequently face higher degrees of academic failure, and also have higher high school drop out rates than their more affluent or suburban counter-parts (Oakes, 2005).

Low performing schools in urban centers are characterized by low teacher morale, high rates of teacher turnover and more teachers teaching without or out of their license areas (Ingersoll, 2001; Ingersoll & Perda, 2010). In New York City, recent numbers indicate that they may have as little as a one in two chance of having a certified math or science teacher (Chanc. Harold Levy, Mach 2004).

In the wake of No Child Left Behind (NCLB) many poor, inner city schools/ districts/systems find themselves in the midst of reform to ensure both improved educational outcomes and continued monetary support from the federal, state and city government. Most of these efforts are forced to conflate educational achievement with standardized test scores, even though many researchers point to the dangers of such unions. In addition to lagging behind in achievement, poor urban students are often not presented with the same opportunities to learn science. They are more likely to have unprepared teachers and have fewer chances to enroll in the advanced courses that are on the college bound trajectory (Ingersoll & Perda, 2010). Other studies indicate that poor students are more frequently tracked into low level science courses in which "good student behaviors" and rote memorization are valued more that the acquisition of dynamic science content, skill and process knowledge (Oakes, 1990).

Still, it would be remiss to suggest that lack of resources is the sole or primary barrier to creating and sustaining successful urban schools. The issue is far more complex and there are a myriad of contributing factors as well as societal forces strengthening the tensions that bound urban education.

For the past two hundred years public education has sought to provide basic skills and instruction in citizenry, morality and the 3 R's. In 1830, the workingman's committee of Philadelphia described the aspiration of the Common School this way, "Our main objective is to secure the benefits of education for those who would otherwise be destitute and to place them mentally on a level with the most favored in the world's gifts" (Tyack, 1967). Essentially, it was believed that the greatest challenge was providing the children of all parents the opportunities to study together. Academic achievement was largely seen as a testament to the will and perseverance of the individual. Over the next hundred years these attitudes would persist and grow more deeply rooted in our culture. Students that failed were thought to be of a lesser moral character or to not have the mental capacity for success. In 1920, the superintendent of schools in Newark, New Jersey argued, "All children are not born with the same endowments and possibilities: they cannot be made equal in gifts or development or efficiency…the educational system must therefore be adjusted to meet this condition" (Deschenes, et.al, 2000).

Rarely, if at all, was instruction, its content or design, considered as a source of student failure. Even more absurd was the notion that the context or construct of schooling was to blame. In fact as the nation became more urban and more students enter the schools, rather than developing a variety of approaches to schooling, what developed was a litany of terminology used to label and separate out those students for whom the system fails. In the early 1800's, these names read "dunce, wrong-doer, sluggish, stupid, incorrigible, and idle", to name a few (Deschenes, et.al, 2000). By the beginning of the 1900's, the list of names had expanded and shifted to include "sub-z group, mental deviates, laggards, average, occupational student, backward, and inferior" (Deschenes, et al., 2000). But, even as we look back at he first century of public schooling, our vision is often romanticized.

We envision the one room schoolhouse as some nostalgic harkening to another time and place rather than examining the harsh realities that it represented for the less affluent family. Students typically only went to school for several months of the year—between planting and harvesting seasons and schools were crowded and under resourced. And although the non-graded culture of the environment allowed students to progress at a pace more in line with individual learning styles, it did little to address the numbers of students who became stagnant in their academic progress or failed to complete school at all (Deschenes, et al., 2000).

By the early twentieth century, members of the progressive education movement sought to challenge some of the political assumptions undergirding the notions of education as a means to equality. They were not prepared to disrupt the notion of the "age-graded" school that in its division of tasks mirrored the ever-growing factory culture that the US was becoming world renown for. But educators were beginning to question the efficiency of educating everyone the same way at the same time around the same subject matter. It was in this era that tracking became a formal part of public education and that we began to use the developing field of cognitive understanding to determine who would study what, and ultimately begin to orchestrate who will have the opportunity to become what (Deschenes, et al., 2000). Put nicely, we began to use aspects of cognition and assessment to remove those students who might slow or retard the progress of the normal student. From a purely efficacy-oriented perspective, this use of our evaluative tools was a smart one. But considering the desire to view school as a tool toward promoting equality among the American public, it must be called into question. What do we mean by equal? And who do we consider to be the citizenry? The waters are further muddied when we take into account the levels of achievement in certain subject areas compared to others, as well as the commodity-like values of certain discipline-based knowledge in the constantly morphing global economy.

When contemplating the purposes of public schooling in the postmodern era we can still place at its core, its role in the assimilation of new cultural groups and students into American culture. Society is told that the education provided can also be a tool to level the playing field and to prepare children of color and recent immigrants for greater opportunities in their future. However, as we review school and school system report cards nationwide, we see that the schools, especially those that serve the traditionally marginalized located in poor urban centers continue to fall short.

Competition, meritocracy and individual accomplishment drive success in American public schools and frame the "democratic" way of life for American school children. For those students living in and/or attending schools in poverty, most of whom are children of color, these values are often in direct opposition to the cultural norms and capital that is most appreciated within their own communities. If we consider, as Coburn suggests, "that a persons' worldview is not just a philosophical by product of their cultural origins, but rather the very skeletal structure on which we hang our flesh of customary behavior", then we must pose the question, "When a child's' worldview is left unvalued and expressionless in an educational setting, what should we expect in terms of engagement, investment and learning from that child?" Boykin insists that some of the cultural inconsistencies between students and schools and teachers may be to blame for student failure and lack of motivation (Lynch, 2000). We extend this argument to include the culture of science as it is taught in schools, from a primarily positivist perspective that suggests its empirical, objective and linear attributes are most salient. We are forced to examine the questions, "What are the goals and purposes of public schools?", "What role does the teaching and learning of science play in attaining those goals?" and finally, "Are schools in poor urban areas designed, organized and allowed to function toward meeting those goals"?

Since the early 1900's educators have continually sought to reform science education. Yet, no matter how or whom, the intent of the reformers has been to create more effective science instruction that leads to more scientifically literate citizens. Put simply, regardless of the students ability to engage or not and experience success or not, we, the members of the educational community continue to allow merely a superficial analysis of our failures in science education and we continue to blame and punish children for them. Our failures, are due in no small part to the curriculum and pedagogies employed in current public school science classrooms.

BUILDING A MORE EMPOWERING SCIENCE EDUCATION THROUGH DEMOCRATIC IDEALS

As the last section suggests, the great democratic legacy of American education has been to create (or at the very least maintain) a sub-class of citizens who are barely learning basic literacy and mathematics skills and are completely marginalized from opportunities to engage in critical, analytic thinking. Schools have regimented their learning such that they have no voice in what they learn, no space to shape the space, topics and process of their education.

And yet, schooling has oft been written about a place where students learn to engage and experience the ideals of democracy (Dewey, 1916; Giroux, 1989; Goodman, 1992). How have the ideals of democracy given way to sub inequality? How might youth come to experience schools in democratic ways when the history of urban science education in American frames youth as in need of fixing, and schools as ways to standardize experience?

Democracy is a challenging word to use in our postmodern world. In contemporary discourse, democracy has come to mean the right to free speech, to vote, a method of decision-making, a political culture, a form of government, an historical perspective, to name only a few referents. Global events, including war, increased deforestation, the collapse of the global economy, has helped to further redefined democracy as a political ideology.

Democratic education has been grounded not in a political process or ideology but in a way of seeking a common good through schooling. The work on democratic classrooms arises from a political literature (Lane & Errson, 2003) and includes a commitment to social justice (Satz, 2007; Rawls, 1971). In the US, the democratic classrooms and schools movement emerged in the late 1980s. Democratic classrooms have been described as "those where all participants – teachers and students alike – have equal right and responsibility to participate in the decision making which frames classroom life" (Apple & Beanne, 1995). Such decisions include curricular scope and focus, classroom participation structures, and rewards and punishments. Yet such rights and responsibilities are much more expansive than decisions around how classrooms activities happen. More deeply embedded in life in classrooms are the social and cultural structures that maintain relations of power among students and teachers. It is also necessarily part of the democratic classroom that the responsibility for shared power and the protection of marginalized voices and perspectives is also elemental.

It is not hard to imagine why democratic science classrooms have not gained much traction. Science teachers working in urban schools face the formidable task of preparing increasingly diverse students from low-income, minority backgrounds for competitive science careers in a high-tech global economy and for citizenship in a world rich with scientific debate. Science teachers facing this mandate are likely to be young and new to teaching. They often are well prepared in science but lack sufficient preparation in teaching in urban contexts to be successful, leading many to abandon the profession because of feelings of failure and isolation. Furthermore, schooling is framed around traditional models of education, where classrooms limit students to being consumers of knowledge who are expected to memorize facts selected as important by their teacher. The traditional relationship between teachers and students leave students with limited opportunities to participate in classroom decisions. In traditional classrooms, teachers are engaged in a power relationship with students in which they profoundly constrain the actions and choices of students. And yet, teachers themselves are caught in a world where they are expected to be the sole authority, both positionally and intellectually.

In addition to these challenges, little attention has been given to what it means to have the right and the responsibility to participate in decision making for either the individual or the social collective in which they take part. One can envision the importance of rights in classrooms by looking at the case of the respect for students' intellectual property, the prior knowledge of science that students bring to the classroom from their cultures and home lives, their "funds of knowledge" (Moll, Amanti, Neff & Gonzalez, 1992). Recognition of students' funds of knowledge is in contrast to common classroom practices where low-income, minority students are seen as deficient in knowledge and skills. To evaluate how teachers value and use students' intellectual property, one can document when and how often curriculum is situated in students' life experiences, home life, background, and cultural and social identities – their funds of knowledge.

While the history of research and development done on building democratic classrooms is important, our concern is more with how we – as researchers, teachers, curriculum developers and assessors – come to understand student participation in science learning and its impact on life beyond school. This book is written to describe frames for advancing critical democracy in science education. What it means to bring student voice into science classrooms in ways that foster critical democracy – not only in how teachers and students enact classroom life together, but also in how students (and teachers) are supported in leveraging their school experiences towards building a more just world?

Specifically, we use the ideal of democratic education in science to call attention to ways of being in the classroom that positions youth as important and powerful participants in their own learning and that of their peers and teachers, and also as members of a larger global society who can leverage their lives in schools towards making a change. We step back to John Dewey to call attention to democracy as "a mode of associated living, of conjoint communicated experience" (Dewey, 1916, p. 87). "Conjoint communicated experiences" seem to be at such odds with schooling today for it calls direct attention to equitable ways of being in the classrooms and moving forth with and through education– a commitment to social consciousness and social reconstruction.

This framing deviates from much of the literature on democratic classrooms where the focus is on how the process of learning itself can become more democratic or in how classrooms can foster deeper understandings of and experiences with democracy. This distinction is important. Democratic classrooms position learning as a dialectic process, where students and teachers learn to "read the word and the world." This means that one both views the world with a critical mindset and envisions how to advance in the world or change the world into a more socially just and equitable place with and through science, while considering oneself as powerful scientific thinker and doer of science.

Thus, the aim of our text is not to provide a "how to" guide to building democratic classrooms. Such classrooms are locally contingent; there is no recipe for designing democratic science education. Rather, we are concerned with the tools that teachers and researchers might use to foster ways of being that lead to conjoint communicated experiences.

DEMOCRATIC SCIENCE CLASSROOMS: VOICE, AUTHORITY AND CRITICAL SCIENCE LITERACY

Consider a girl, who attends middle school in the poorest congressional district in the country, and is failing science in the fall of 6th grade, but then builds a strong relationship with her science teacher through caring for animals in his classroom during recess and after school. He leverages her animal caring experiences to position her as a science expert during science class. She moves to an A student and refers to herself as "a science poster child." The experiences that students bring to the class-room and how they are able to voice them towards the creation of empowering science education matters.

Consider another girl, whose has struggled with school attendance and success but who also considers herself a "make a difference expert" because she helped to design and collect over 200 surveys on the local community's energy practices, analyzed them in excel, and presented the findings to the mayor's energy policy council, who then made changes in how they distribute recycling bins to Lansing residents. Youth are experts and working with them to author transformational authority matters in building a more just world.

Consider a middle school boy, who likes math but wants to open a t-shirt shop when he grows up. He does not know what engineers are or what they do, and his mom is worried if her son gets too much into science and math he may get picked on. Yet, after conducting an energy audit in his school along with his classmates and at the local university with energy engineers as a venue for delving deeper into energy transformations, he decides he wants to become an engineer, maybe, one day. Becoming science literate is both about knowing and becoming.

These three stories are real and have been made possible by teachers and students working together to enact a more democratic science education. Our understanding of democratic science education is grounded in critically oriented sociocultural perspectives of learning, which describe learning as a situated process shaped by the social, cultural, and political environment in which it takes place. As people learn, they move from a peripheral participation in the subject matter community towards a more central position in which they become a fundamental part of the decision and rule-making processes (Lave and Wenger, 1991). These perspectives suggest that learning ought to be thought of as an ongoing process of participation and identity formation, in which learners acquire what is needed for participation in relevant communities of practice, while they construct what kind of people they are and what they aspire to be (Wenger, 1998). In this process, students negotiate forms of participation and identities within the rules and expectations of the worlds they participate in as they engage in their daily practices (Lutrell, 2001).

In this book we draw specifically upon three core conceptual tools that help to frame ways of thinking and being in classrooms that work towards a more just world: Voice, Authority, and Critical Science Literacy. While we briefly describe each conceptual tool below, we note that these ideals are taken up in different ways across the subsequent chapters.

Voice

Student voice is not a new concept in education but it is centrally important in democratic science education. Student voice captures the ideas that students' opinions and ideas matter in both the perspective they hold and in the actions they take (Calabrese Barton & Furman, 2006; Mitra, 2004). Indeed, recent educational research has shown the positive outcomes of school programs aimed to foster youth voice, including teacher learning, reforming school and teaching practices, and for the participants themselves. Tobin and his colleagues have extensively worked with student researchers through cogenerative dialogues that both support teachers in more critically reflecting upon their teaching and learning to incorporate student ideas into their teaching (Tobin, Elmesky & Seiler, 2005). Others have utilized student researchers as well in schools. Fielding (2001) demonstrated that when high school students researched school issues that they identified as important with the goal of providing recommendations for school change, transformative school practices emerged such as the incorporation of students to the evaluation of new curriculum.

At the same time, student involvement in school improvement has also suggested that the incorporation of student voice is transformative to students themselves. Elmesky (2001) reveals how youth gain empowerment through science by having opportunities to expand upon and embrace their embodied resources, like deep knowledge of hip hop. In describing this stance, Elmesky describes in rich, contextual detail the ways in which she has involved youth as student researchers. Participating students had opportunities to expand their own science toolkits by virtue of participation in the project, and teachers and researchers in this study had their own views challenged and deepened by the youth.

Clearly, voice matters. The science education community does not have a deep understanding of what urban youth experience, potentially care about, or the non-traditional resource they access or the ways that they may activate them. Further, student voices provides active and meaningful learning experiences similar to Dewey's (1890) notion of "transformed recitation," which he envisioned as students providing their experiences and ideas and dialoguing with teachers in order to set up new lines of thought and inquiry. Critical visions of education have further claimed that student voices allow children to create their own meanings and become active authors of their worlds, demanding thus that students assume a proactive role in the planning, implementing and evaluating of their own learning (Freire, 1971; Giroux, 1988; Simon, 1987).

Despite these calls, student voices still do not fare well in many American schools: Whether spoken or written, they have too often been reduced to lifeless, guarded responses– responses to the questions and assignments of powerful others, responses formed in the shadow of teacher scrutiny and evaluation. Given the fate of student voices, it is difficult to believe that traditional schooling contributes to the flourishing of individuality and democratic decision-making (Lensmire, 1998, p. 261).

Shared and Transformational Authority

In education studies, authority is often framed through reason or position without deeper consideration of how such positional authority is situated within cultural and social norms that can be oppressive (Pace & Hemmings, 2006). This perspective distinguishes authority based on how one is endowed with institutional power by virtue of their status (position) and knowledge possession (reason). In the case of teachers, authority is assumed based on status and knowledge where teachers have "authority both in the sense of having the power to direct classroom activities, and in the sense of having the knowledge that the students need to acquire" (Buzzelli & Johnston, 2001, p. 875). The authority of position and reason are particularly compelling in science class because science disciplines are usually taught and perceived by teachers and students as having "well-defined, unequivocal answers and solutions, as well as the unambiguous rules that students typically encounter in the exact and biological sciences" (Raviv et al., 2003, p. 19)".

The limitation of this perspective on authority is that a "school's preoccupation with the authority of reason and of position can cause teachers and students to ignore a type of authority lying at the heart of action and performance: the authority of experience" (Munby and Russell, 1994, p. 97).

Our work with youth suggests that although the authority of position and reason play out in powerful ways in school science – and that one must be attentive to how it gets constructed, there are other powerful ways in which youth purposefully seek to enact authority in schools in ways that are transformative. Indeed, we have witnessed youth who have sought ways to enact their own authority against the tide of position and reason. As minorities living in a majority-controlled society, coming from low income families, and students in schools that do not appear to value their experiences and knowledge, many of the youth we work with have not been perceived as possessing authority based on position or knowledge. These students were neither in authority, nor authorities themselves.

Democratic science teaching employs a different slant on authority and its relationship to classroom communities. We refer to this kind of authority as both shared and transformational. In this framing, authority is not based on position but rather on how and why one leverages knowledge and experience towards bringing about social good. Here, we recognize authority as relational, and bound by social and cultural structures that define relationships. It is enacted or exerted *directionally* – with particular goals in mind, though such goals are not always conscious. What contrasts this kind of authority with the authority of position and reason is the idea that all individuals possess authority because it is formed and informed through the continuous and interactive nature of experience rather than an institutional hierarchy or an epistemic truth. This authority that we describe here is similar to Pace & Hemmings (2006) idea of emancipatory authority or "authority that serves the education of all students as well as the democratic values of justice, the common good, participation, and the freedom to question" (p. 26). However, it also calls attention to the role of students in the process and in the desire to use personal and scientific knowledge and experience towards change.

Critical Science Literacy

A number of authors have explored the idea of scientific literacy, producing various definitions of this concept (Laugksch, 2000). There have been growing debates on whether the science education community's focus on science literacy should also explicitly incorporate notions of citizenship and democratic participation (Hobson, 2003). It is argued that schools could be more centrally concerned with "civic" science literacy (Miller, 2002), which focuses on (1) scientific understandings of basic foundational ideas like matter and molecules as well as on the nature of scientific inquiry, and (2) the development of a regular practice of consuming science information through reading about and evaluating scientific ideas as they relate to the public sphere. This view of science literacy is not drastically different from those ideas put forth by Project 2061 (Benchmarks for Scientific Literacy, 2003) when this project first introduced "science literacy" to the science education community's lexicon in the 1980's. However, the emphasis (or balance) between "what" one should know and "why" this knowledge ought to be taken up in daily life differs in civic science literacy, with more emphasis on how and why public consumption of science ought to take place.

Despite calls for science literacy or even civic science literacy, it has become common knowledge that most pupils in the US school system fall short of this goal. Both Project 2061 and National Science Education Standards (National Research Council, 1996) argue for a stance on literacy and science that combine content, inquiry skills, and habits of mind but do not necessarily offer insights into how a powerful combination of these three critical areas ought to frame participation in a democratic society. While both of these major policy documents carefully state the importance of conceptual understandings in making sense of human action and interaction, little attention is given to what this might mean or look like. Science should be taught in a manner that "inspires student understanding and enthusiasm, and is relevant to the cultural and social needs of students and society" (Hobson, 2003, p. 110). We believe Hobson advances how we ought to be thinking about science literacy; his point, however, stops short of engaging the idea that learning is about agency, about transforming one's world.

Learning, thinking and knowing involve "relations among people in activity with, in, and arising from the socially and culturally structured world" (Lave & Wenger, 1991, p. 51). Yet, not all situations are equally valued. Thus, any instantiations of science literacy must also attend to how "situations are themselves confluences of widely distributed streams of activity" (Nespor, 1997, p. 169). Indeed, part of science literacy is a process of developing a critical consciousness with respect to context, with the power to transform reality, positioning the learner as a growing member of a community, with expanding roles and responsibilities (Freire, 1970). From the perspective of democratic science education, science literacy must therefore be attentive to the roles that youth generate or accept for themselves within science-related communities, their reasons for participating in particular ways, and the relationship they perceive these roles have to the knowledge and practice of science. Here we view these articulations of what it means to be successfully engaged in science (i.e., successful science learners) as both products of and contributions to one's location in the world.

We refer to this kind of science literacy as critical science literacy because without access to the content, practices, and discourse of science, youth may not have opportunities to develop rich repertoires of science knowledge and practices for engaging in the world in empowering terms. Yet access alone does not account for how youth might learn to understand what science is, to utilize science for personal and social transformation, or to engage in public discourse and debate. Critical science literacy not only promotes all important elements of science literacy as advocated by the American Association For The Advancement of Science [AAAS] (AAAS, 1990) but it also embeds essential skills to participate in a democratic society in fair and just ways. Instead of just attending to "what" individuals need to know, critical science literacy challenge the socio-political context of how and why youth are taught to engage science in the current system, thus challenging the functional view of science literacy that promotes economic growth at the cost of poor and marginalized groups (Calabrese Barton & Upadhyay, 2010).

KATE AND HEATHER: WORKING TO INCORPORATE VOICE, AUTHORITY AND CRITICAL SCIENCE LITERACY

To help illustrate our points, we present two stories of fairly new science teachers, Heather and Kate, and their attempts to enact student voice, authority and critical science literacy in their science classrooms.

Kate

Kate was in her second year of science teaching. After trying out different career options as a computer engineer she had gone back to school for a masters degree in education because she wanted to make a difference. She chose to work in New York City despite having grown up in the suburban south because she felt this was where she might be able to give the most. Pivotal to her decision where her own high school experiences:

> In my high school, it was a magnet school, but it was — it put the magnet school in a high school because the high school had low scores and a large, low-income, minority population. And so they put a magnet school in to make — to bring up the school, but in my classes, I mean, my classes were not mixed. Our graduating class, the high performing students, were all magnet kids from other cities, and so I saw that, and I thought, "This is messed up." And I don't know, I thought there was so much room for improvement in public schools already, so that's what I wanted to do."

Kate believed that school science was about bringing together "knowing and doing" in ways that would both open up opportunities for youth in their future lives but also help them in the moment. Making these in the moment connections were important to Kate because she felt that this what would help her students see the relevance of science. Her students were not only members of groups who have been historically underrepresented in the science, but also the students in her school had not, as a set, fared well academically in science or other subjects. She wanted her students to feel inspired by science, to use science to critically question their life experiences, and make solid connections between home and school. Science was the natural subject area to make connections because as Kate said you can make science out of any problem.

Yet Kate acknowledges that learning science in ways that promote critical literacy, connections, and inspiration is challenging, especially when you are not insiders to your students families or communities. After her first year of teaching she realized that she did not have all of the "answers." She acknowledges a big "ah ha" moment that fundamentally transformed her teaching. During a unit on forces and motion, Kate introduced motion probes to the students so that they could measure and graph the movements and velocities of small cars as part of their lesson. When she first introduced the probe wear Kate seemed surprised to see that the students wanted to play with the probe wear rather than use it to conduct their assigned experiment. Instead of getting frustrated with what appeared to be "off task" behavior, Kate made an "on the spot" decision to modify her lesson. She told the students they could conduct whatever motions they wanted in front of the motion probes and record their data, that they would talk about later that day. They would conduct the experiment the next day. Many of the students could be observed dancing in front of the probes, laughing, and recording their dance movements graphically with the probe wear data. While the class did get back to the car experiment, it took 2 days rather than one because of the level of interest students expressed in understanding the physics of their dance movements. In speaking with

Kate after the lesson she said she was surprised she hadn't thought that the students might simply be excited to use the probes since they had never been introduced to the technology before. She also said that she learned a valuable lesson that day – that even reform minded curricula grounded in the students' experiences may still not really capture your own students' experiences. As teachers you have to constantly be paying attention to the cues that your students give you.

Student voice mattered a great deal to Kate but so did allowing them to have epistemic authority in her classroom. In her second year of teaching, Kate had called a parent to discuss the students' lackluster grades. When the parent suggested that her son would be interested in doing a science fair experiment, Kate decided to design a science fair for the entire school. The fair, she felt, would meet both the needs of the District Exposition Project and to provide students an opportunity to share their work with the school and neighborhood community. Kate decided that the crux of the science fair project would be an experiment: Each student would conduct their own investigations and present them in the standard demonstration format for the school to view. She wanted the students to have authentic projects but she also wanted to offer her students structure, given that they had not participated in such an event before in that school.

Kate offered three organizing structures to support students in developing their projects:
– A list of experiments the students could select from, based on her own research into experiments that were "inexpensive" and "simple" and could be measured or rated or quantified.
– A guideline for preparing the research paper and poster.
– A series of worksheets aimed at helping students through each of the primary steps in their investigation (i.e., developing a hypothesis, designing the experiment, etc.).

After offering an initial week's work of intensive instruction/activity on the science fair projects. She also provided one class period a week for about 9 weeks to allow students to work independently on the project while also having access to school resources. The science fair was transformative for both Kate and the student, Quacey, as we describe below.

Quacey, who was relatively new to the country (his family having moved from Ghana 1.5 years previous), spoke with a marked accent, and was well liked by his teachers and his peers. Though students sometimes made fun of his "big lips," Quacey was tall and confident and used those qualities to win and maintain friends.

Quacey loved to build. His father is a construction worker and one of his brothers is a construction worker as well. He says that in his free time, he takes out all his toys, which are mostly screwdrivers and motors, and builds cars. Quacey was also rather articulate about the science behind the things he built, typically drawing upon his experiential knowledge to explain how things work: "Well the [car] motor, uh the motor got like magnet inside of it… It like a magnet… it got metal around it and it got magnet and it got like this thing inside…"

The first weeks' work on the science fair was marked by Kate reviewing with the students what a good science experiment was and the guidelines for the project.

She handed out the list of experiments to choose from and gave students time in groups to investigate the list and to settle on an idea. She also offered the students a worksheet to guide them through how they would transform the research topic into an experiment. However, despite his intense interest in doing a science fair project, Quacey was unsatisfied by the list because his topic of interest was not included; he wanted to build something and he was keenly interested in space exploration. When he explained this to Kate, she responded by saying, "then come up with a proposal!" Quacey and his partner first sought approval by presenting their topic – building a Mars Rover – to Kate, in both written and oral formats. They demonstrated a connection to a topic previously studied in class (forces and motion) in a way that validate their topic and showed it as worthwhile and scientific. In their discussions with their teacher they referenced the classes previous study of the Mars Rover, a topic his class briefly covered months earlier during a NASA rover rendezvous with Mars. They also presented written evidence for scientific sources of information they could draw upon (i.e., NASA website and science books), and they showed knowledge of key science ideas involved (i.e., pressure and lift off, H2 as fuel, and electricity) (see figure 1.1).

They also framed their building project as a design experiment, by offering a hypothesis that the rocket would "vibrate and the light would be flashing and the perpeler [sic] will spin" when it moved across the planet surface (see figure 1.2).

While Kate conditionally accepted the boys' idea, she was firm in her resolve that their project needed to be adapted in order to be "more experimental" – in other words, she wanted them to be able to offer evidence that their rocket or rover was a success or failure. As a result, Quacey and his partner continued to

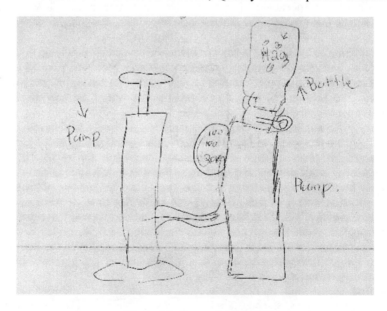

Figure 1.1. Quacey's rocket design.

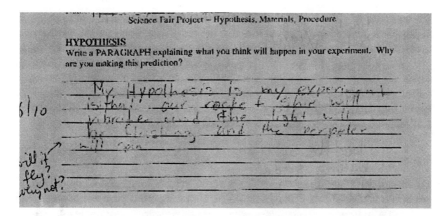

Figure 1.2. Quacey's hypothesis.

negotiate aspects of their project to maintain the support of their teacher (i.e., how to frame their project as an experiment) while holding to those dimensions of their project most important to them (i.e., building something). They adapted two key teacher suggestions: they referred to their Rover as a "model" and they modified their protocol to include multiple tests in order to offer quantifiable data. They also decided upon two different models in order to compare data that would allow them to build two different designs.

As a result of these strategic negotiations, Quacey and his partner were able to maintain an emphasis of their project on building but at the same time learned to view building as a process of design and experiment, and they created an opportunity to educate the rest of the class on this topic. They were able to keep as central their identity as builders but also continued to be science students in good standing. Through the topic of building they were able to validate their efforts to draw upon nonschool-based resources for completing the project, including parental expertise on building and using the internet, parental views on aspects of science that are important, personal experiences building, and social alliances for drawing in various forms of individual expertise (i.e., the group expanded to four students, and one person was the artist to create the final model sketches, another the lead builder, while two others the researchers and writers).

In other words, they found a way to balance the school expectations, knowledge or resources with their individual interests. They used the project to have their interests a valued and official part of science class, to build and maintain the kind of social relationships that mattered to them, and to still be viewed as smart and scientific by their teacher. They were lucky – One possible reason why they were able to co-opt this science event is that they had a teacher who wanted also to value what they brought to the classroom and was willing to "negotiate" with them to make it happen in a way that met her needs and expectations as teacher.

It is no surprise that in setting up the guidelines for the science fair that Kate bounded the science fair assignment by requiring students to conduct an experiment, rather than allowing them to make a model of something, like a volcano, which is often observed at science fairs at this grade level. The science fair "had to be about" solving some problem or issue. It was also not surprising then, that Kate also came up with a set of "research projects" that students could undertake that directly related to the content covered in school that year. Before she introduced the science fair to her students, I (Verneda) observed her spending hours and hours researching the content covered in the school that year so that she could provide students with examples of projects that connected this content to her students lives. She ended up distributing a list of research questions that students could select from based on her research.

Heather

Heather was an 8th grade science teacher at the School for Social Change (SSC) in New York where she has taught middle school for five years and particularly developed a materials science class which draws on current topics in physics and chemistry. SSC is a small public school that opened in the Sunnyside Park neighborhood of New York City in September 2004. It was part of a second-wave of small new schools opened with the approval of three authorizing agencies – New Visions for Small Schools, the Gates Foundation, and the New York City Department of Education — as well as a series of other non-profits such as the Annenberg Foundation and the Open Society Organization.

The school opened with seventy-five sixth-graders and seventy-five ninth-graders; now, the school serves 525 students, ranging from grades six to twelve. The school is housed in a campus that it shares with four other small schools; the existing large school in the building has been phased out.

Heather was drawn to SSC because she had flexibility and freedom in how she taught. She even referred to the school as having a culture of democracy. She situated her class in what students thought, though she would generally design the framework for what happened in class. She saw SSC as a place where she could visit other teachers' classrooms to learn. One thing she hoped was to personalize to individual students the content and skills she normally taught.

Heather believed that democracy in a school prepared students to be active citizens, and in order to be active citizens, they should vote for order of units, the type of final project, and the type of field trip to take. She also thought they could help with classroom management. Thus, as a teacher, Heather is deeply conscious of the importance of incorporating student voice in her classroom as well as sharing authority with the students.

In the fall of 2007 and spring 2008, Heather put a new set of democratic teaching ideas into action. First, as a prelude to this project, Heather and her students independently wrote and/or drew their conceptions on how democracy fits into a science class. Second, she and three of her student helpers (Dale, Kristy and Trisha) polled her class for a science activity they would most enjoy in the future, and designed a plan to enact this idea. Then, Heather and the students designed a contract for participation during dissection and a worksheet that would support students in learning a variety of anatomy and physiology while dissecting the frog. All of these processes involved Heather's three student helpers and the voices of students in her different science sections, making the entire process democratic, in that it included subject knowledge but also student experiences and ideas. Her students were co-constructors with Heather of both the expectations and climate for the science classroom, as well as the science projects they wanted to engage in.

The class had chosen frog dissection as their preferred activity even though the course covered the realms of physics and chemistry. They wanted to step away from their regular classroom activities for a day and act like "real" scientists conducting an investigation. It was also something the students were very interested in doing, and Heather was supportive of their decision. In addition to designing how the activity would proceed in class, Heather and the students also identified their roles in the classroom and designed an assessment to figure out whether this type of activity had influenced their peers' engagement and long- ad short-term interest in learning science.

From exit interviews and analyses of the assessments that the participants crafted, many students in the class in which this dissection happened learned about frog anatomy, physiology or evolutionary history – all of which they were able to communicate. The participants themselves seemed to most benefit from the experience of planning and executing the lesson. Their knowledge was refined and they had good ideas about how to dissect and also how to help their peers in this process.

For example, students in exit interviews made some the following comments: "One thing that I noticed is that frog parts are similar to human anatomy. That suggests to me that humans and frogs may originally have come from a similar place." In a community where evolution is not a popular explanation for species diversity this comment particularly stands out as an important marker of learning. Several students talked about the idea "of adaptation" and how animals like frogs develop body parts suited to their environment. This is an important evolutionary concept that students will need to know in high school. Students learned a variety of new dissection skills that would help them in future activities in high school labs, e.g. one student talked about having the flexibility of using the scalpel, while others talked about their surprise when they cut into the frogs and there were different layers of texture before diving into the inner anatomy. Two features the students found particularly fascinating were the nictitating membrane on the frog eyelid and the reverse attachment of the frog tongue. This was definitely new knowledge and provides a new example of how student choice can lead to peers engaging in high-level detailed observation. In addition to knowledge of laboratory safety and procedures, Heather reported the following as New York state 8th grade science standards she addressed with her students through their lesson:

> Standard 4
>
> 1.1g Multicellular animals often have similar organs and specialized systems for carrying out major like activities.
>
> 1.1h Living things are classified by shared characteristics on the cellular and organism level. In classifying organisms, biologists consider details of internal and external structures.

This is an example of how Heather's students were gaining critical science literacy – learning rigorous scientific knowledge that they were invested in.

A few students commented that the frog activity "really" made them feel like scientists because they were actively doing and exploring and they had independent choice. It made them feel as if they were acting like scientist, a field in which Heather's students are vastly under-represented at all levels. Heather's students were able to enact and experience critical science agency, both in being a confident scientist from a minority background and in shaping one's classroom. New roles for certain students were also created so that authority is shared between Heather and her student-helpers. Heather said: "Even students who would lose focus because of what other students were doing around them would eventually come back to their work without too many reminders from me.

However Heather's students helped choose the topic of the day, organized its outline, made sure the material was content-rich, provided clear safety guidelines and reserved spaces for student choice in the activities. This process was critical because student power was integral to the design and execution of the day. The roles and reactions of the three students are described below.

Heather reported that "It made me realize that I can have students helping one another out; being "teachers" more often and it could be productive," suggesting that the experience shifted her view from that of a classroom where teachers kept knowledge and power to students supported to be experts could have shared authority with teachers, to the benefit of all students. Heather's story described how a teacher can create many routes to democracy in her classroom, how this environment empowered youth in "critical subject agency" – deep knowledge, more engagement, challenging under-representation, and tackling issues of equity and power through subject knowledge. The goal was to show how democratic science teaching creates a hybrid between traditional and progressive educational practices and a third space in which low-income, minority students can experience success, voice and choice in their science learning.

LOOKING AHEAD

In Kate and Heather's classroom we see, in her collaboration with students, elements of democratic teaching emerge in that she shared authority with students, cultivated student voice, and sought to support students in bringing their "funds of knowledge" (Moll, Amanti, Neff & Gonzalez, 1992) in choosing their activity, and challenged traditional classroom power structures by being flexible and student-centered in her teaching approach. Building student voice into her classroom, sharing authority with youth, drawing on students' lived experiences, giving students structured choices were central to her identity as a teacher. In a world of standardized test pressures, poor pay and classroom management challenges, co-creating her science class with students helped Heather keep their needs and interests at the forefront of her priorities. Because she cared about what students want and think, youth were often in her classroom at lunch and after-school and tried to excel at the complex scientific knowledge- and inquiry-based tasks she posed to them. Likewise, Kate demonstrated sensitivity towards student interest and voice, taking their ideas and suggestions seriously in both the probes activity and science fair projects.

With Kate and Heather, we can see how these themes of community and shared authority are important to her teaching. Perhaps more important is why these goals matter to them and to the teachers in the following chapters. As discussed before, critical science agency continues to be a key theme in a model of democratic science pedagogy. In Heather's classroom as in the ideas presented by both groups, students acting as agents of change as the goal of democratic science pedagogy—shaping what happens, what is taught and how teaching and learning occur. Students' had authentic opportunities to engage science in ways that validated their voices and perspectives. In her class, a significant and formative factor in her classroom practice was that students took on more equitable standing with their teacher and had more voice in the curriculum and structures of their classrooms.

Schooling can be viewed as preparation for real-life but what that means is that students are expected to conform to normative standards. Young people spend so much of their time in school and this context shapes so much of their intellectual and social lives—it seems only respectful of their time and experience to consider school an important space that they can shape in their own image.

Democratic science pedagogy has the potential to shape learning outcomes and science engagement and that these possible impacts are worth exploring. Both teachers and students in this study either demonstrated or articulated enthusiasm for science classrooms reframed from a democratic context as holding the possibility of bringing out the best in students: motivation, a desire to learn, an energy for being engaged in science content and classroom debate. Further exploring the nature and impact of democratic science teaching has the potential to address issues of social justice in science education and science itself by empowering teachers and students in traditionally marginalized urban schools to craft science and its instruction in ways that feel meaningful and relevant while opening doors for students to success and engagement in science courses and careers, and helping students develop science knowledge, which they can use to make change and redress power differentials in their lives.

OVERVIEW OF THE BOOK

The book follows the following structure. In Chapter 2, Jhumki Basu interrogate what we might learn about equitable and empowering teaching by listening closely to youth. The chapter draws extensively upon the experiences of two of Jhumki's students and their work in her high school physics classroom to offer a more expansive lens for the outcomes of science education. This chapter specifically takes on the construct of "critical physics literacy" to argue that the learning outcomes of democratic and empowering science teaching should include not only deep under-standing of the knowledge and practices of science but also a science identity that fosters critical engagement in science towards building a better world.

Chapters 2, 3 and 4 delve into the processes and outcomes that frame democratic science education: agency, authority, and empowerment. In Chapter 3, Tara O'Neill examines the relationship between student ownership of science and student agency. As Basu does in her work on critical physics agency, O'Neill calls us to examine more carefully what science learning communities look like such that they foster authentic ownership of ideas. In doing so, she makes a case that agency in science is a more powerful measure of student learning because it positions youth as producers and users of scientific ideas, rather than merely consumers.

In Chapter 4 we interrogate how youth purposefully merge their everyday discourses with those of science in order to transform what it means to be an expert in science – making critical to expertise the ability to talk across communities of practices in ways that are meaningful to the members of different communities, whether it be scientists or neighbors.

Chapter 5 takes us back into classrooms to look at how elementary children appropriate democratic practices in science teaching and use them to form their own instantiations of empowerment and what it means for teachers to recognize these in public ways. Each of these chapters provides us with a rich snapshot of youth-in-action, taking the reigns to illustrate to others what it means to be an empowered learn and expert in science.

Chapters 6 and 7 return to the question of teaching and the role of leadership. What can and do teachers do to foster empowering and equitable learning environments among their students, and how are these practices culturally situated. In Chapter 6, Gale Seiler presents the story of a young pre-service teacher in post-apartheid, rural South Africa who sought to redress issues of injustice in his science classroom by enacting specific teaching strategies including incorporating ESL language teaching strategies and incorporating cultural congruence. In Chapter 7, Christopher Emdin addresses the ways that the concept of citizenship, through the use of cogenerative dialogues, coteaching and cosmopolitanism (The three C's) as a triad of tools, can improve student experiences in the science classroom and provide students and teachers with the agency to address inequity both within, and beyond the classroom.

Finally, the last chapter, Chapter 8, examines cross cutting themes across the text and focuses on how to re/frame the problem spaces of equitable and empowering science education.

JHUMKI BASU, ANGELA CALABRESE BARTON,
NEILE CLAIRMONT AND DONYA LOCKE

2. YOUTH VOICES

Challenging the Outcomes of Science Education

In this chapter, we present the experiences of two of Jhumki Basu's students and their work in her high school physics classroom to offer a more expansive lens for the outcomes of science education. This chapter specifically takes on the construct of "critical physics literacy" to argue that the learning outcomes of democratic and empowering science teaching should include not only deep understanding of the knowledge and practices of science but also a science identity that fosters critical engagement in science towards building a better world. This chapter is based upon her publication in Cultural Studies in Science Education.

About half way through the school year, the students in Jhumki's ninth-grade conceptual physics course were presented with an opportunity to co-design a lesson for their class. The option was voluntary, but the teacher presented the opportunity to all of her students as one way to incorporate students' voices and experiences in her planning and teaching of physics. One student, Donya, took up the challenge because, as she described, she wanted to connect what she was learning in her physics class with her interest in becoming a lawyer, and she wanted her peers to be able to make similar connections. Donya initially told Jhumki that for her lesson plan she wanted her peers to engage in a class debate on the gravitational pull of black holes.

In describing her reasons for selecting the debate format and this topic, Donya cited a past experience from physics class, where she and her peers argued about the impact on the world of Einstein's $E=mc^2$ equation. Donya was excited by the idea that a high school science student could take a position on important scientific ideas and could argue about the impact of an idea developed by someone as famous as Einstein (See Figure 2.1 in which Donya is describing her perspective on debate in science). She also liked the idea that debates on controversial topics in science do not necessarily have right and wrong answers but that they require students to develop and defend a stance. Donya thought that if she set up a debate then her peers would have a chance to think through ideas instead of repeating back what their teacher construed as the "right" answer. Donya thought that a debate would better prepare her for her future as a lawyer. She also engaged in a sophisticated view of science as tentative, rather than a canon of static truths.

With help from Jhumki, Donya expanded her debate from a focus on the gravitational pull of black holes to include the impact of dark matter and energy on

*S.J. Basu et al., (eds.), Democratic Science Teaching: Building the Expertise to Empower
Low-Income Minority Youth in Science, 21–40.*

Figure 2.1. Donya discussing the role of debate in science.

the future of the universe. Donya wanted each student to take responsibility for understanding the material, so she instituted a requirement for each student to write a paper on the topics of dark matter and dark energy during the week leading up to the debate. See Figure 2.2 for examples of material that Donya and Jhumki created together for the debate.

On the day of the debate, Donya acted as the facilitator and judge. Based on research they had conducted in response to questions such as: "What do scientists think dark matter is?" or "What is the evidence that the universe is accelerating apart?

Court Room Trial of D... Matter and Energy:
A Modern Physics Trial

Co-Designed by Donya Locke

Structure
- **Trial Monday 6/6**
- Tues 5/31 – research paper, Wed 6/1 – pool research, Thurs 6/2 – prepare for trial, Fri 6/2 -- **practice preser   ions**
- 2 courtroom trials
- 2 teams per trial: one defending, one prosecuting
- 6-7 people per team
- Judge and jury made up of students and teachers evaluate the team
- Winning teams get a pizza party (we know we owe you one already!)
- Counts as test for this unit

Timing (40 minutes total, 5 minutes t sition to next debate)
1. Opening Statement Team A (2 mi...
2. Opening Statement Team B (2 min)
3. Main Arguments Team A (6 min)
4. Main Arguments Team B (6 min)

5. Preparation for Rebuttal – both teams (5 min)
6. Rebuttal (Response from Team A) (5 min)
7. Rebuttal (Response from Team B) (5 min)

8. Closing Statement Team A (2 min)
9. Closing Statement Team B (2 min)
10. Judge and Jury Evaluation (5 min)

Trial Question
Dark matter and *dark energy* have been accused of pulling apart the universe so that it will become a cold, distant place without life and light. Is there evidence to convict *dark matter* nd *dark energy* of this crime?

Figure 2. Handouts for the debate created by Donya and Jhumki.

Cadero
Donya Slehom
Jhumki

Court Room Trial of Dark Matter and Energy:
A Modern Physics Trial

What is dark matter? How does it affect the universe?	Team explains what dark matter is	Team explains □ what dark matter is □ why scientists came up with the idea of dark matter	Team explains □ what dark matter is □ why scientists came up with the idea of dark matter □ how dark matter affects the universe
What is dark energy? How does it affect the universe?	Team explains what dark energy is.	Team explains □ what dark energy □ why scientists came up with the idea of dark energy	Team explains □ what dark energy is □ why scientists came up with the idea of dark energy □ how dark energy affects the universe
Convincing argument	Team does not have one strong opinion. People in the team are disagreeing with each other and not working together. Evidence is weak.	Team has a well-thought-out opinion but makes **mistakes** in the evidence they provide, or the evidence is convincing.	Team is inspiring and convincing in their argument. They provide lots of **EVIDENCE** for their position, not just opinion.
Presentation	Team members could not be heard. Team members were confused about what they were saying.	Team members had prepared but read from their papers. Speakers did not make eye contact. Presentation had not been practiced.	Students spoke clearly and with energy. Team members could speak without reading. They made eye contact. Main points were clear. Presentation showed signs of practice.
Level of research	Team seems to have conducted very little research. Team is just sharing their opinions *or* what they learned in class	Team seems to have done research but but did *not show* **how they** used **sources**	Team explained what sources they used and **how they used these sources,** either through a poster or at the end of their main arguments

Figure 2. Handouts for the debate created by Donya and Jhumki. (Continued)

How convincing do you think this data is?," teams of students presented pro and con arguments for whether dark matter and dark energy were pulling apart the universe. Each team had five minutes to present an opening statement and then faced five minutes of questioning from the other team followed by a few minutes to respond to questions. At the end of debate, students voted on what they thought was the best answer to the debate question.

Donya created rules of conduct for the debate, for example: "No put downs such as 'Your argument is stupid'" and "You must raise your hand if it's not your time to speak." She also created a rubric for the debate, which she and Jhumki used to evaluate whether the groups participated in the debate, how respectful they were to other teams, and the level of detail and specificity of answers in their written report. For example, one criterion in the rubric was: "Team is inspiring and convincing in their argument. They provide lots of evidence for their position, not just opinion."

Despite what Donya and Jhumki considered to be detailed planning, Donya felt that the debate was unsuccessful. In her particular ninth-grade section, she felt that the students were not as actively engaged as she had hoped. Within groups, there was confusion as to who was speaking and in what order. Students did not seem to understand how to link the content they had learned on dark matter and energy to an evidence-based stance on how these shape the universe. Donya's observations of these problems inspired her to envision ways in which class could be altered to better support students in learning to make arguments. For example, she felt that the ninth-graders might benefit from public-speaking lessons. Also, Donya thought that students needed practice with small group debates before engaging in a full-class debate.

The following year, Jhumki incorporated Donya's debate in her ninth-grade physics class. When she prepared students for the debate, she used Donya's suggestions. She had students discuss what it means to speak well in public and had them practice presenting their stances to each other, prior to the final debate. The students also took on personas of religious leaders and physicists, which helped them engage in the idea of interpreting information from different perspectives. Far more students participated successfully in the debate that year, as a result of Donya's reflections on how to support students in debating complex, controversial science topics.

Donya's experiences helping to set up a class debate on dark matter and energy are a glimpse into how she helped to create a place of engagement in school science that supported who she was and wanted to be. Donya made use of the opportunity to plan a lesson in collaboration with her teacher to experiment with the idea that learning science was not always about right and wrong answers, but could also be about arguing science ideas, in evidence-based and reflective ways.

The vignette about Donya suggests that she was an agent of change in how her physics class was structured. Freire (1970) argues (and we agree) that a primary purpose of education is to support students in becoming agents of change. Change is an interesting concept because it could mean larger social change or smaller incremental change. In the case of Donya's experiences crafting a debate on dark matter, we see, if for a moment, a young woman who begins to understand what it means to think and know scientifically and to use the opportunity of lesson planning to help her peers to see that too. Given that school science for many youth is an experience in getting right (or wrong) answers, Donya sought out significant changes in how science is learned, albeit on a small scale in her personal classroom context. Donya certainly experienced challenges in enacting her lesson – things did not turn out in the ways she had planned. But her reflections on what went wrong moved her and her teacher to better understand how students learn and what supports they needed to engage debates.

For Donya, and for other students in our larger study, their experiences in physics simultaneously engaged them in content knowledge and education for change, or what we refer to as "critical science agency." In this chapter, we investigate when and how students developed "critical science agency" in a physics context and what this meant for their deeper engagement in physics learning.

STORIES OF DEVELOPING CRITICAL SCIENCE AGENCY
IN A PHYSICS CONTEXT

We begin this section with Donya's and Neil's stories of critical science agency. For both students, the story is their own personal narrative, which they wrote themselves. For authenticity purposes we leave their narratives in the first person, but italicize them to offset them from the rest of the text. The purpose of these stories is to introduce the readers to the participants, as they describe themselves in their own words. Following the vignettes we reflect upon their stories to unpack what critical science agency can look like in a high school ninth-grade conceptual physics classroom.

Neil's Story

My name is Neil, and I attend the School for Social Change, which is located in Brooklyn, New York. I am an eleventh-grader. During my freshman year of high school at the School for Social Change I met this wonderful teacher named Jhumki. She taught me science for two years in both ninth- and tenth-grade. Jhumki came to me one day and asked me if I would be interested in robotics and the New York/ New Jersey Robotics tournament. My first response was "No. I won't be able to build a robot. It's too hard "Then after two-three weeks I told her "Yes, I would love to learn about robots." And from there my future and goals were to build robots for the military and Homeland Security. My main goals were protecting soldiers and finding terrorists. Robots can improve the life of my fellow comrades dying in the combat field. My cousin served in Iraq for one year which was very painful not only for him but for his parents. However after high school I plan to join the army. "Hooahhh!!!"

Besides joining the army I have many other goals I want to achieve in the near future. I am a student who is very interested in robots. I have participated in the New York/New Jersey Robotics tournament for 3 years now. My teammates and I came up in the top 10 in the competition where we had a big challenge to face ahead of us.

I also learned about robots through the ninth-grade science fair. The ninth-grade science fair was something I will never forget because the science fair showed and taught me a lot about how seriously I take robotics. For the science fair I built a robot that went back and forth (see Figure 2.3) *with a mechanical claw attached to it, without any remote control – just in respond to its surroundings, based on a*

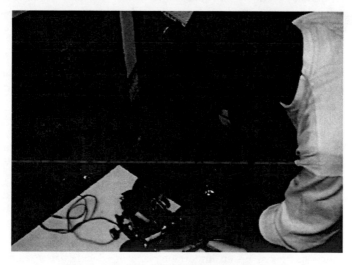

Figure 2.3. Neil and his robot at the ninth-grade science fair.

program I downloaded from a computer into the robot's brain. The skills I have learned with regard to robots are to build a powerful robot that will be able to move around and is aware of its surroundings. I have learned to attach sensors so that the robot can be alert regarding what's in its sight and programming in Virtual C, which is a very difficult thing to do. The reason why it's difficult to do is because you must write the correct program in order to have a very successful mission for the robot. (Any slight error will cause the robot to fail its mission). I increased my programming skills by taking a two-day workshop that introduced me to the robot before the first year I started the competition and by reading a manual on programming and playing around with the programs.

Donya's Story

My name is Donya Locke, and I am about to become a senior this year at the School for Social Change. I am the type of student who likes to be challenged and I find no joy in doing work that is fairly easy. I tend to get very frustrated when I know right off the top of my head what I am supposed to do. I like to think of myself as a strong and intelligent person. Therefore I often try to go beyond my ability. I set certain goals for myself that I try my hardest to accomplish. I also love to get involved in many different activities. I feel that my brain takes me beyond where I should be and that's a good thing.

Since I was in Junior High School, I have never been a big fan of science. However, I try to get involved with various aspects of it because you can really realize that it's very interesting. At this point, I am linking even more because it's growing on me, which helps me understand it better.

In my ninth-grade year I created a science lesson for my peers. For extra credit I helped my physics teacher plan a lesson on black holes. The purpose of this lesson was for the students to learn more about dark matter and more specifically black holes. It was also an opportunity for them to be able to argue for and against the topic. At first I did not know what I was doing but I used my career goals to help get through it. When I grow up, I want to become a lawyer so what I decided to do was have a debate. One question was "If any object ever gets sucked into a black hole will it be able to get out?" So we split the classroom into two groups, one side said no and the other said yes and they had to use research to prove why they are correct. In this lesson, my role was the facilitator and the judge.

The classes did very well however they had trouble using the information they had as arguments for the other side. Another set-back was that students chose not to participate but instead kept their heads down and were quiet after entering the room.

CRITICAL SCIENCE AGENCY AS AN ITERATIVE AND GENERATIVE PROCESS LINKED TO IDENTITY AND THE STRATEGIC DEPLOYMENT OF RESOURCES

Defining Critical Subject Agency

Critical agency has taken up an important place in educational research framed around research on issues of equity and social justice. Whereas the vast majority of research on critical agency tends to focus generally on students' abilities to build critical awareness and engage in acts of social transformation, a subset of this work is more deeply grounded in how participation in *subject matter communities* frames one's enactments of critical agency. For example, in a study of urban sixth grade mathematics students, Turner and Font (2003) characterize *critical mathematics agency* as viewing the world with a critical mindset and engaging in action aimed at personal and social transformation through developing deep and rigorous understandings in mathematics.

Next we look across both stories to describe how critical science agency in a physics context emerged as the expression of identity and the strategic deployment of resources and identity.

Neil. Neil's story in this study begins with him arriving from St. Lucia and struggling academically and socially in his school. It unfolds with him taking on ever- expanding challenges in physics, computer science and engineering, building relationships with teachers and students and establishing himself as an expert and agent of change at his school.

Neil's story suggests that the expression of critical science agency – Neil identifying himself as powerful science thinker and doer in ways that advanced his participation in his community – was connected to the expansion of his identity (taking on the roles of expert and teacher and building social networks with peers and adults). In Neil's story, we begin to see how a young man worked with his teacher to create opportunities to expand his knowledge of robotics, and have that knowledge mean something for his conceptual physics class. In the process of doing so, he was afforded opportunities to draw upon his deep understanding of robotics, electricity and forces and motion, to build a new identity in his science class as an expert in robotics, and to use that knowledge and identity to transform some aspects of his own life and his physics classroom.

Neil—an expert in robotics. In the weeks before the science fair, Neil sat at the back of class at a table separate from his peers. Each day, he spread out across the table the parts of his robot and a dedicated laptop and worked on either building the physical structure of the robot or programming its movement. Students visited his construction area/design site during these weeks to look at his robot as it developed and to ask him questions about his next task. He rarely spoke in class except to ask his teacher for help with his work. This was in sharp contrast with Neil's usual behavior – prior to the science fair unit, he often moved about the room, participated in name-calling and arguments with his peers and his teachers, sometimes stared and rolled his eyes at students, burped loudly in class, and called out unexpected and often rude comments. In an interview, Neil described his behavior as a purposeful decision to "act dumb."

Learning programming required Neil to develop expertise. He had to read from manuals, test out sample programs, and spend hours trouble-shooting with his physics teacher and with mentors at the local university that sponsored the robotics competition in which he was involved. Revising his robot time and again taught Neil to build a strong, self-contained robot.

27

Neil's experience with robotics also helped to reinforce some of the concepts covered in his conceptual physics class. As he constructed his robot, Jhumki observed Neil review and enact schematics that involved concepts about electricity such as charge, current, voltage, resistance, diodes and more. For example, he studied the circuit board associated with his robot and identified parts of electronic circuits. He had to find batteries of different voltages for different appliances. In his science fair poster, Neil displayed his attempts to craft the kinds of programs he had wanted to create for his robot and the challenges that he faced in this process. He provided this information as an example of hypothesis-testing through data collection in that he tested programs he thought would work and modified them based on his results. In this sense, Neil gained literacy not just in physics content but in the open-ended inquiry aspect of being a scientist.

On the day of the science fair, Neil placed his robot in the hallway on top of a game board he had drawn on a portable white board. When Jhumki came to look at his project, there was a crowd of students around him watching him run the robot as it collected colored plastic pieces and pushed them into the "trash." Neil noticed the buzz he created. He said of the science fair: "a whole bunch of people came over to my group and wanted to see bunch of things... They wanted to see the robot move." Two scientists who acted as judges during the competition later told Jhumki that they felt his project was of a quality distinctly higher than those of any of his peers. Neil won first prize in the science fair competition, based on the evaluations of several ninth-grade judges. When he told Jhumki about his feelings about winning the prize, he said: "The day of the awards they [the students] were like, 'Neil, Neil, Neil.' I know it's me. The students say 'We all know it's Neil getting awards.' I was like, 'Yeah it's me, why not?'"

Neil had profound interest in computers and robotics, fueled in part by his desire to invent new technologies to save the lives of soldiers in war. These interests, in many ways, propelled Neil into the role of capable physics student and expert. Not only were these changes reflected in his grades in the course but also in his developing identity as a capable school science expert. What is interesting is that despite the expertise Neil demonstrated in robotics and computing, he was not initially viewed by his peers or teacher as a good science student or an expert in physics. This is important because it suggests how easy it is to underestimate a student's potential, based on his/her behavior in class, and how exploring a student's interests and talents is an essential part of developing a young person's critical agency.

Neil—a robotics teacher. A powerful aspect of Neil's story is the way in which he cultivated and drew deeply upon his physics knowledge to position himself, over time, as an expert *teacher* who acted as a learning resource for his peers. Through physics, Neil altered how his peers viewed him, by presenting himself as a knowledgeable and serious student who could help them make connections between their lives and physics class.

During interviews for this study, Jhumki asked Neil to develop ideas for a lesson. Neil also chose to enact his ideas for teaching robotics with the whole class. He based his lesson on his experience with the robotics competition at a local university for which he had prepared and in which he enjoyed participating. He said of the competition: "I met a lot of people at the tournament, teams that came over and helped us with programming. The people at the tournament, I liked them 'cause they respected me."

Over the course of the year during which this study was conducted, Neil spoke with his teacher several times about when and how he could build a game board, the kinds of equipment we could order for the in-school robotics competition he envisioned, and the kinds of funding we might acquire for materials. A year after Neil designed his unit, he and his team-mates had a chance to co-teach robotics with Jhumki as a unit of the "Medicine-Engineering" course offered to tenth-graders.

Jhumki chose the robotics kits the students would use, primarily based on the budget that the school allocated for the class. However, Neil and team-mates previewed the robotics kit before it arrived. Then they prepared the materials needed to run the robotics class: they unpacked equipment, figured out what types of batteries were needed, downloaded the software for programming onto ten laptops and sorted the Lego pieces for students to use.

Prior to each lesson, Jhumki would discuss with Neil and his team what they might do in class. The topics of the lesson mostly aligned with what Neil envisioned: constructing stable structures, exposing the students to various types of sensors, having its program and preparing students for an end-of-unit competition. In describing what he taught, Neil said:

The lesson was teaching students about robots because I did robotics. I liked it and I think all the students will. The first thing I be doing is introduce the topic, talk to the students about what robots means, what different things robots can do, what different parts of a robot are useful – touch sensor, light sensor – to start the robot. I tell them what it is used for. Then they write an evaluation – if Neil was a good teacher for the day or not. [I tell them] what different hydraulics can do, open and close, how to build claws.

In class, Neil moved between groups to help students solve building problems and become familiar with the software program. If during class, students struggled with programming or communication between the computer and robots, he came at lunch to try and sort out the problem, so next day's class ran smoothly. Neil also helped collect and organize materials at the end of class. At one point, Neil recognized that all of the robotics team members were in one section of the medicine-engineering academy and none were in the second teacher's classroom. Neil felt comfortable enough in his expertise to volunteer to be a student teacher in the other classroom, where he would not have access to Jhumki's supervision. Neil designed the final game board for the competition on his own; in this sense, he created the parameters for the final assessment of the unit.

Neil's interest in robotics and experience in physics allowed him to take on a new identity as a teacher in his classroom.

Neil—building social networks with peers and adults. Neil's participation robotics afforded him more than knowledge of how to build and operate robots. This experience put him in contact with other students and adults who either shared this interest or wanted to see him succeed with it. Figure 2.4 depicts the strength of

Figure 2.4. Neil with team-mates and his father at the university robotics competition.

relationships Neil developed through robotics. The image captures the photographs from his university robotics competition that he considered important enough to gather together for presentation at the science fair. In the pictures, you can see that Neil has shown his team-mates working and posing together as well as a photograph of him with his father in which he describes his father as proud of him.

Building a strong social support network was important as Neil struggled with the transition to high school. He struggled with his grades and to cultivate positive relationships with his peers and teachers. The context of science provided Neil an opportunity to cultivate new relationships. Both the science fair and the co-teaching experience led Neil to expand his network of resources, including new adult relationships and new knowledge, upon which he could draw for doing robotics and computers. He regularly worked with and e-mailed two mentors at the local technical university sponsoring the robotics competition and found a summer internship at a robotics lab through materials he acquired from these mentors. He continued working with Jhumki over the next two years on his robot, setting and achieving goals for expanding his robotics skills until the 11th grade science fair. In 11th grade he even met with Jhumki's husband and father, both of whom were computer programmers, to discuss programming his robot and to design business cards that captured his ability and desire to fix his classmates' home computers.

Seeking out this adult help and mentoring reflected what was may have been a turning point for Neil. Despite Neil's initial struggle with classroom behavior, he began to find spaces through physics to build a network for success. He also began to project an identity as someone who was smart in this area rather than as someone who "acted dumb." In physics class, Neil noticed the stature he could acquire by engaging in high-quality work: He said, "I do get respect sometimes when I do my work. Because when they pass me, they ask for help." Neil also expressed his appreciation of the friendships he built through robotics.

The cohort of "friends" Neil made on the robotics team provided him with a social network that he maintained for the next three years. He organized a "going-away" party for one of his team members when this friend left for Trinidad at the end of Neil's junior year. He also could be found meeting regularly with these friends and Jhumki. to discuss how to improve science teaching and learning for urban youth, even when Jhumki was not his teacher.

Agency and identity. Because engaging in agency involves reflection and the development of awareness, it necessitates that individuals continually examine their identities – who they are and how they change. Issues of identity – and how one positions oneself (or is positioned) through practice and identity building – are central to making sense of how one seeks to pursue one's goals. In our use of the term identity, we align ourselves with those who view identity as fluid and constructed socially within communities of practice. Upon entering a community of practice such as the science classroom, students develop identities through engaging with the tasks of the science class. Learning science becomes "a process of coming to be, of forging identities in activity" or "identities-in-practice" (Lave & Wenger, 1991, p. 3). For example, how novice members of a community negotiate their relationships with the official authority, that is the science teacher or the recognized good science students, shape not only the goals students may choose to pursue but also how they identify with that community and its goals.

Bringing this framing of identity to bear on agency, we take the stance that the process of *coming to be* is rich with agentic possibility. As Holland (1998) argues, based on their particular "imaginings of self" (p. 5), individuals, as part of a process of agency, set particular goals towards which they want to direct their action. Evolving identities-in-practice can be inferred from the way students choose to interact with other members, the decisions they make with regards to the assigned tasks in the science classroom, the opinions and questions they raise and also their reticence and silence, should they choose not to participate. Holland (1998) writes of agency as a form of "semiotic mediation – modifying one's environment with the aim, but not the certainty, of affecting behavior" (p. 39). Embedded within is the idea that pursuing agency does not guarantee a particular outcome but, instead, requires risk-taking, through which one might expend energy but not achieve one's goal.

The relationship between Neil's identity and agency. In physics, Neil leveraged the aspects of his identity that compelled him to pursue robotics such that he could build a new social identity for himself with respect to peers and adults. He expressed agency in that he used his experience in physics to change his life. Specifically, he positioned himself as a socially-connected expert and modified the world of his school by instructing other students in robotics. Overall, Neil's critical science agency was deeply connected to leveraging and expanding his identity. He drew on his passion for computers and robotics to develop as an expert, teacher and socially-networked young man.

Donya

Donya's story in this study begins with her as a strong, motivated student interested in a career in law. During the student she explores challenging topics in physics such as black holes and dark matter and energy. She also tackles a unique, difficult science fair project. By the end of the study she positions herself as a scholar and expert who can guide her peers and as a young woman who challenges stereotypes about urban minority youth in science. She also says that she is more open to the possibility of a career in science.

Donya's story suggests that the expression of critical science agency – expressing herself as powerful physics and scientific thinker in ways – was connected to her identity as a student and helped her expand her identity (such that she established herself as an expert student and scholar challenging what she saw as stereotypes about black students).

Donya—an expert student and scholar. Donya was a student who wanted to challenge herself. She applied these qualities in physics to expand her knowledge and scholarship, further developing her intellectual identity.

With regard to black holes, Donya began her investigation of this topic by intentionally choosing the most difficult of three topics for a first semester project on motion: how a moving object might avoid being drawn into a black hole. However, she did not feel that she had "learned everything" about black holes through her first semester project, so she decided to do more research on this topic in designing the lesson she chose to enact in Jhumki's class. For her lesson, she studied topics as diverse as the density of white dwarves, the process of fusion, the formation of collapsed stars and the speed of light. Clearly, Donya sought out a depth of physics knowledge through the design of her lesson. Because Jhumki wanted students to learn about a topic other than black holes, since some of them had already encountered this idea for their first-semester motion project; Donya went a step further in her research by agreeing to conduct research on the topic of the lesson to dark matter and energy, a new topic for all students, instead of on black holes. She established a scholarly identity in this area by writing a paper on this subject, based on research, which provided the foundation for questions students should research for the debate. Donya also drew on her identity as a future lawyer to bring debate into her physics class.

By leveraging her desire for challenge and innovation, Donya also expanded her identity in the realm of scientific inquiry. She wanted to pursue an "original" project for the science fair, "something different" from what her peers were examining. She arrived at the idea of exploring how objects float, and she chose as her partner someone whom she thought would work hard, despite the fact that this student was not her regular partner and best friend. She viewed this partner as "someone who will really commit to doing this project with me and really complete it."

In agreement with how Donya said she normally sought out challenge, she described how she struggled with the number of hypotheses she was expected to generate for the science fair but enjoyed the new experience of conducting her own experiment. She said she liked "getting to check the results and test ideas in different ways." During the science fair, Donya enjoyed being independent. She liked knowing where she was going with her work, to the extent that she could start work right away without waiting for her teacher's instructions. She said, "In the three weeks, we knew what we were doing, we would just go to it."

During the science fair, Donya and her friend displayed a detailed poster describing their experiments with floating different objects of different shapes and sizes in different types of liquids (oil, water, soda, etc.). They presented their findings on a detailed poster board documenting their scientific process. About the science fair, Donya said that she felt "really good, I felt we were doing something really extraordinary. It felt like we were in an art museum showing off our work." She also took pride in a comment from a judge that described her project as "original," different from the types of experiments other students had pursued.

Based on her experience with the science fair, Donya decided to further explore science. She said: "All in all, this experience has taught me a lot and I feel that I have started a new beginning because now I'm starting to think that I may like to pursue a field of science in college which is something I never thought I'd do." The summer after her sophomore year, Donya enrolled in a nanotechnology course for high school students at a local university while also attending a pre-law program.

Donya—challenging stereotypes about black students. Donya relied upon this physics context to critically thwart the negative stereotypes that abound about black youth and the economic discrimination often seen in black communities. While Neil began to see a different future for himself through physics – one that allowed him to safely step out from "acting dumb," Donya used physics to shield her aspirations from and challenge a racialized world. Donya's involvement in physics demonstrated critical dimensions in that she explicitly challenged, through her actions as a science student, stereotypes about low-income, minority youth in science. As she states: "My name is Donya, I think the reason that most areas, black areas lack funding because...they think black people are just going to be the ones who work at McDonald's, that' why they don't give us funding. They think it's a waste of their money." Through her decisions to challenge herself with the toughest science projects and as evidenced by her position on her school's honor roll for every semester that Jhumki has known her – by leveraging her identity as a strong, capable student – Donya purposefully demonstrated that urban black students could be in a position to be excellent science students.

The relationship between Donya's identity and agency. Donya expressed agency in that she changed her own life by positioning herself as a scholar and guide to other students and modified her world by creating a space in which students could debate scientific ideas. Donya's critical science agency was related to the development and expansion of her identity. Her commitment to challenge and innovation allowed her to expand her identity as a scholar, science inquirer and someone who challenged stereotypes about urban minority students.

Critical science agency and students envisioning their futures. Neil's and Donya's experiences with critical science agency indicate that this process was deeply connected with the leveraging and expansion of identity. In metalogues on this topic, Donya and Neil raised the point about identity but in a way that connected not only to who they are but who they want to be. This looking ahead on the part of students further emphasizes how taking action toward shaping identity is important to how these students frame their participation in science.

> Donya: Science is more exciting to me and the whole class when the teacher structures a class around who the students are, or want to be.
>
> Jhumki: Like wanting to be a lawyer.
>
> Donya: Like being a lawyer. What is in science for me is that with the lawyer thing, there were a lot of topics that you could discuss that would be practice for being a lawyer. It's not just how you might argue your point, even though that matters. It's also about seeking out good evidence, and making it fit together to make a point. And it is also about asking hard questions that do not have obvious answers.
>
> Angie: Donya and Neil, your stories about becoming a lawyer and a robot expert are telling me that part of what is important in helping you learn science is being open to how science intersects with not only who you are now but also your futures. In other words, developing a critical science agency is about developing an identity with and in science.
>
> Neil: I think it is important for teachers to remember that students have goals that science can help us achieve, and that these goals are not always the same as getting a good test score. Sometimes these goals are really connected to the science we might learn. For the class I taught, it related to robots, which I want to do for Homeland Security. That class I taught also helped me how to understand how to program the robot, also open up my mind and set me on the correct path of what I want to achieve. But sometimes these goals are not really connected to the science directly. Like the science fair reflects on me, because I came in first place, and through the science fair, it shows what I can achieve. It helped me realize the goal that I want to achieve.
>
> Donya: Learning science for me is about doing something. I mean its just not doing hands-on stuff because the debate is also doing something. I mean that learning science is also when you can do things that you develop yourself, like Nicolas said.
>
> Jhumki: And so I need to see your learning, or at least part of your learning, in my class as about how you are able to build your future?

Neil: You know, it is not just how things directly tie to my future. I enjoyed learning about black holes even it wasn't my topic. I learned a lot about black holes and I also learned about what Donya wants to be in the future. Why did she care about that? How did science class help her? If she wants to achieve in science to help her be a lawyer maybe that is something that I haven't thought about. This is different than just learning what an atom is.

Critical Science Agency Involves the Strategic Deployment of Resources

Neil's strategic deployment of resources.   Neil's initial interest in robotics was related to his concern for the well-being of American soldiers in Iraq. Throughout the year, he drew on resources inside and outside of school to expand his knowledge and experience and pursue his goals with respect to robotics. These experiences include his participation in an inter-school competition at a local technical university, choosing a robotics project for his science fair and participating in internships with the school computer expert and as a computer-use advisor to patrons at a local library.

Neil also drew on human resources to pursue his critical goals. For example, during the science fair, he came to school early, worked in Jhumki's office at lunch and stayed late to build and program his robot. The week before the robotics competition, to improve his robot, Neil visited his mentors at the local technical university everyday after school for several hours. He relied on his peers as a resource in establishing himself as a robotics expert, relying on their help to co-teach his robotics unit with Jhumki

We consider Neil's deployment of resources to be *strategic* because he purposefully drew upon both traditional and non traditional resources in ways that positioned him with voice and authority, and in ways that challenged and even transformed normative and stereotypical rules for participation in science by urban youth. In our metalogues with Donya and Neil, Neil stresses how this strategic leveraging of resources is really a negotiation of who can participate and how that participation is made to matter to the larger community.

Neil: I think we have to include the other students in this negotiation, too. The kind of help I needed was a game board, which was a really big game board that my father built. And the robots competed against each other. And another help I needed was my friends gave me ideas, of where to put the different pieces on the game board – not this way but the other way, and they gave me feedback on where to put the different objects. I also got help from you on how to make the unit more organized so students know what they're doing and would like it and could learn something from it even it wasn't their topic. Cheef and Darius helped me because the programming was too hard to make the robot go forward, backwards, sideways. I needed help to make a claw, to put the pieces together to make a strong and powerful robot. They helped me a lot.

Jhumki: In addition to students, the larger context shapes this negotiation. Neil, do you think you would have been so involved in robotics if there hadn't been that New York Robotics competition?

Neil: Yes, it was important. Because I met people and got to see what new people can do. Such thinking was very brainy, and I got to see it, the other students at the competition. The mentors they also gave you feedback, this part is right, this part is wrong, the program.

Angie: It seems to me then, that central to any negotiation – whether it be about identities, futures, content, or context – is a process of opening up and coming to know.

Donya's strategic deployment of resources. Donya drew upon the context of physics to expand the repertoire of resources she could access and activate towards her own goals. We can see her goals coming into sharper focus as a result of her deployment of these resources. Donya's expressions of and reflections on agency were dialectically related to context, rather than being limited to her own individualized experience. In her assessment of her dark matter/dark energy lesson, Donya suggested structuring debates based on her experience with the E=MC^2 debate and on classroom formats she had seen in end-of-year exit projects and during her visit to a local college. In choosing how to improve the debate the following year, she drew on the experiences and attitudes of her fellow students. In reflecting on her science fair, she drew on the comments of the scientists who had come to her school to judge her project. We consider Donya's deployment of resources to be *strategic* because she purposefully drew upon both classroom and beyond-school resources in ways that positioned her as a scholar and expert and in ways that challenged traditional stereotypes about urban black youth in science.

Teacher as resource in critical science agency. Donya and Neil pointed out in their metalogue that they also significantly relied upon dialogue with their teacher as an important resource in this negotiation.

Neil: From my opinion, teachers should speak to the students and have their voices heard, have the kids say how they think class should be organized, how it should go along. Teachers should listen to what students have to say – students are the ones who are learning, not the teachers! As a teacher, you tried to help me achieve me my goals by having me, as a student, come and teach in the classroom. It helped me learn new things I never knew about and learn more ideas about how to help people."

Donya: Jhumki, you gave me the idea of being the lawyer.

Jhumki: I did? I thought you were thinking of being a lawyer?

Donya: I mean, you helped me connect being a lawyer to black holes and to doing the debate. You helped me see how science class can help me achieve my goals.

Jhumki: So it sounds like our conversation one-on-one was helpful.

Donya: Well, I could not have done it on my own because what you told me
to do was to make a list, write down what I needed to get this done.
Having this in front of me made me see, yah, that is me. That is what
I want to do. But then to think that black holes could help? I mean
that is really true.

Jhumki: So you could lead class when I didn't just tell you to lead class or
I just decided to do class. It was that you had your ideas, and I knew
some things, and we worked together. I could help you make a list.

Developing Critical Science Agency is an Iterative and Generative Process

We use the term *iterative* in this chapter to mean that a person constantly re-
evaluates and modifies her knowledge and identity. By *generative* we mean that as
a person expands his knowledge, his sphere of interaction, and his influence grow,
allowing him to further access and activate new forms of capital.

Neil's critical science agency as iterative and generative.   Neil's experience with
critical science agency was iterative. He regularly wrote, tested and then modified
programs to get his robot to perform in the ways that he desired. For example,
Figure 6 shows his conclusions about how to make a robot turn, a conclusion he
developed from a series of trial and error steps with robot motors. He taught his
peers new ideas for building and programming, and had them test those ideas while
he was there to help them.

   Neil's experience with critical science agency was also generative. His success
with the science fair helped him develop his understanding of robotics while
expanding his stature as a serious, smart student. His presentation on robotics
during his end-of-year portfolio project established himself as a teacher of robotics.
Both these experiences expanded his confidence and supported him in feeling
excited and assured about teaching a full robotics unit to other students. These
also inspired him to seek out internships in computer science and robotics outside
the familiarity of his school setting, which in turn encouraged him to develop his
robotics project further for the ninth-grade science fair. Over time, his behavior in
physics class improved as did his willingness to rely on Jhumki in situations where
he needed academic, personal or professional support, for example, seeking out
Jhumki's father in designing business cards or Jhumki's husband for fixing his
computer and developing a theory of programming.

Donya's critical science agency as iterative and generative.   Donya and Jhumki
engaged in an iterative process when Donya developed her debate lesson. Jhumki
asked Donya what kind of lesson she wanted to create; Donya discussed how she
very much enjoyed the Einstein debate, in light of her interest in law, and said she
wanted to pursue a debate. She chose a debate topic that appealed to her desire
for challenge and originality, tapped on her experiences with her peers (particularly
what she saw as their tendency to rely on one group member for completing work),
and helped her fill gaps in her knowledge of black holes. Donya also suggested new

teaching practices that were very useful to Jhumki in designing debates by evaluating her experience with the debate she crafted. So, in Donya's experience with critical science agency, Donya re-evaluated and modified both her knowledge and identity. She even expanded her career aspirations to include science.

Donya's critical science agency was generative in that she developed new expertise about black holes, dark matter and dark energy. She also expanded her sphere of influence by working in a partnership with Jhumki, rather than simply being a recipient of the pedagogy Jhumki crafted. For example, Jhumki and Donya worked together to streamline the debate topic and traded rubrics, debate instructions and research questions for students back-and-forth, in designing the lesson. Eventually they debriefed about the success of the lesson, and Jhumki used Donya's suggestions in her class the following year. Donya also established herself as a leader (teacher and judge) with respect to her peers, a social position that was important to her.

Donya's and Neil's metalogue reflections on how critical science agency was iterative and generative for them. We end this section on the generative and iterative nature of critical science agency with a brief metalogue with Donya and Neil because they summarize for us how learning to participate in physics and to use such participation to bring about change is transformative not only of their identities, but also of what it means to be successful in high school physics. Their actions changed their positioning in school science because they took on new roles and because we learned to respond to them in productive ways.

Neil: Well, what I know is that she did care, and my life is different now. I can be brainy and that is OK. I really don't know how I would have been if Jhumki did not care. I would still be doing robotics, but it would not be in my physics class. Maybe I would still be skipping class.

Donya: At the beginning of ninth-grade, I didn't like science, but I learned new things about science. Now, I'm even thinking of becoming a scientist. I'm a person who likes to be challenged, and I don't like to know the answer right off the top of my head. I like to do research and have a scientific experience. Like with the debate. It gave me a different aspect of science. I didn't know science had something that could go both ways. And I liked that part. But, it has changed me, and that matters for me both inside and outside the classroom.

Jhumki: And that change has taken place and makes sense in both of your worlds inside and outside the classroom.

Neil: And in the future. In ninth-grade, I did my first robotics competition and I went off to do it in class, and then I went off to doing an after-school program at New York College, and then I went off to doing a robot program at NY Technical School, making a robot that works underwater, and then I got second place at the eleventh-grade science fair. And I couldn't do the programming, and I kept getting better and better. Like in my spare time, I would work on programming and then it would work, but back then I just got started. You know, I did not try to become a better student on purpose. I acted dumb because it was part of me. But robotics has a purpose to me, and having that taken seriously gives me a place to be who I am and who I want to be. Being a good student is not following classroom rules. We shouldn't talk about good students or even good teachers, but good science learning because that is how it happened for me.

CRITICAL SCIENCE AGENCY & DEMOCRATIC CLASSROOMS

In Donya's and Neil's stories we see two valuable points about critical science agency that both parallel and challenge each other. First, Donya used the context of physics to develop an identity as an expert physics *student*, who was both original and hardworking, whereas Neil used the context of physics to develop an identity more so as a specialized robotics expert and a *teacher*. Donya used her good social standing and school smarts, her hard work ethic, a sophisticated view of science, and confidence in taking risks to challenge stereotypical images of who can be successful and what it means to be successful in science. This differed from Neil, who drew more from adult networks, non-traditional knowledge, and a shared interest in robots to support his identity development.

Despite the difference in how their critical science agency played out in light of Donya's and Neil's different identities, our findings suggest that the expression of critical science agency for both youth was connected with their intellectual and social identities and the strategic deployment of resources. In addition, for both, the expression of critical science agency was an iterative and generative process. How these resources are either made available in classrooms or recognized and sanctioned by teachers is thus an important feature of empowering and democratic science education. Critical science agency supports youth in developing a kind of expertise that matters in their own lives – in how they build a sense of self and seek to interact in the worlds they traverse. Such situated expertise cannot necessarily be predicted before hand by a teacher. Thus, building opportunities for students to voice and act in such ways matters. This is not to suggest that teachers cannot lay claim to what their students ought to know. Indeed, critical science agency and subject knowledge are not at odds. In fact, an important aspect of expressing agency for both youth was the development of their physics knowledge in the context of their identity. Donya conducted research on a controversial topic in modern physics and applied it to her aspirations for a career in law and her quest for challenge and originality in her education. Neil became a robotics expert, and through this, established himself as a potential robotics developer and a scholar and teacher at his school. In their metalogue, Donya and Neil associated a positive physics experience with the development of knowledge. Donya felt that choice gave students the incentive and opportunity to better understand a topic. Neil felt that exposure to a robotics competition gave him "smart" ideas; this was a way to build his repertoire of robotics knowledge.

The iterative, generative nature of critical science agency is also an important feature to consider in building more empowering and democratic classrooms. In an accountability climate, there is a sense of immediacy for urban minority youth to perform. For example, students and schools are often considering to be failing if test scores do not show a specific kind of progress. But the findings of this study suggest that the development of science expertise and engagement with science take time and ongoing human interactions. Neil became an expert by revising his work over time and building one opportunity in robotics upon another. Donya worked in conjunction with Jhumki to revise the plan for the following year. So the study suggests the need for longer-term metrics for understanding how low-income, minority youth learn science, with attention to their human interactions and the resources they leverage.

Key resources for the two youth in this study were in-class (physics curriculum such as the Einstein debate), out-of-class (end-of-year portfolio presentation), beyond-school (local university competitions and field trips), material (game board and robotics equipment) and human (teacher-student dialogue) resources. Donya and Neil, in their metalogue, also emphasized the importance of one-on-one teacher student dialogue in pursuing critical science agency. The findings suggest the importance of youth being exposed to a diverse world of opportunities that allowed them to create networks and mentoring connections in- and beyond- school.

Critical science agency, we believe, is an important construct in advancing our understanding of empowering and democratic science education. Clearly, the boundaries used to frame what it means to be literate in science are too narrow to fully grasp how both Neil and Donya grew as science scholars and youth who make a difference. The relationship between knowing and doing was not limited by traditional classroom activity, but was made more intense by the inclusion of out of classroom and out of school activity and an eye towards the future. If we had used traditional measures to make sense of either Donya or Neil, we would have a deficient view of their experiences in 9th grade physics. We may see Donya as a superior student – straight A's in physics, good attendance and class participation. But Donya, in a sense, is at once more astute and fragile than her report card suggests. She worried deeply that her lesson plan failed, yet wanted her peers to know that science doesn't always have answers. We may see Neil as a student on the verge of either passing or failing – skipping class, disruptive behavior intermingled with moments of success in the science fair. But Neil is much more cerebral and committed to his future than we might otherwise know. A framework of critical science agency, which requires us to understand that what students know is intertwined with who they are and want to be, has pushed us to develop more complex understanding of both youth.

TARA O'NEILL

3. IMPROVISATION WITH/IN SCIENCE

Expanding Worlds and Lives

In this chapter I share stories of working with youth in an after school Technology Club to create movies about science in their lives. I use these stories to argue that an important aspect of empowering science education is valuing the role of student agency as both an outcome of the learning process and as a generative contributor to the on-going re-design or transformation of the learning community and of the self. This work draws specifically upon Dorothy Holland's framing of agency, which defines agency as being when and how individuals or groups act upon, modify, and/or give significance to their worlds in purposeful ways, with the aim of creating, impacting and/or transforming themselves and/or the conditions of their lives (Holland et al., 1998). Embedded within this view is the idea that agency is built upon a critical awareness of one's world and, in the case of agency in science education, a deep understanding of science and a desire to make a change in one's life as a science learner (see Basu's work on critical science agency, chapter 3).

DEFINING AGENCY IN THE VIDEO PROJECT

There is more to learning science than learning content. Science learning, particularly in any transformative form, is a combination of learning content, developing skills to think critically about science content, and being able to activate one's critical awareness of science and her or his environment in order to intentionally effect change. The enactment of agency is done in an effort to create positive change in one's "figured world". This change must occur at both the individual and social level, as a person's "figured world" is constructed by the combination of what the individual believes to be her or his reality and how others acknowledge and respond to that reality.

Agency is tightly linked to identity through a dialectical relationship (Holland et al., 1998). Identity refers to ways in which one participates in the world and the ways in which "others interpret that participation" (Brickhouse & Potter, 2001, p. 966). Holland's vision supports this notion of identity existing on both personal and social levels, arguing that "identity is a concept that figuratively combines the intimate or personal world with the collective space of cultural forms and social relations" (Holland et al., 1998, p. 5), such that a individual holds multiple identities at the same time. In its most simplified form, a person's identities exist simultaneously within two spaces. First, there is the individual's perception of self. This would be

S.J. Basu et al., (eds.), Democratic Science Teaching: Building the Expertise to Empower
Low-Income Minority Youth in Science, 41–54.
© 2011 Sense Publishers. All rights reserved.

the space that Brickhouse (1994) and Holland et al. (1998) refer to as the "personal world". The second space is the social world. This is the identity formed by the individual's awareness of other's perceptions of themselves (Brickhouse and Potter, 2001).

Holland et al. (1998) argue that there are two forms of the agency – identity dialectic: Symbolization and Improvisation. Symbolization is when an individual relies on the objectified identity or objectified figured world (as represented through symbols) to direct self and others actions. Improvisation refers to the process when an individual is in a contested or ambiguous space and the individual uses her or his resources creatively to change the norms or routines of the figured world.

Improvisation is a particularly powerful and transformative form of the agency – identity dialectic because rather than using the norms (i.e. objectified identity or objectified figured worlds) to direct one's actions, the individual takes action to change the norms. As Heble (2005) describes, "improvisation can encourage us to take new risks in our relationships with others, to work together across various divides, traditions, styles, and sites to foster new models of trust and social obligation, and to hear (and to see) the world anew. It can facilitate new kinds of global and intercultural conversations, and it can serve as a powerful marker of history, memory, identity, difference, and community" (n.p.).

The student participants of the Technology Club's video project drew upon improvisation to alter their figured worlds within the video project and their everyday lives. In the context of the space of the Technology Club, where the requirements of the project were ambiguous and under negotiation, the students' agency was in their ability to use the resources available to them to change the direction of the project in effort to gain access to new resources and ultimately altering their figured worlds. This stands in stark contrast to their classrooms where ways of knowing and being were highly regimented and students had little influence over what was taught, when or how. While this project takes place in the informal spaces of schooling, the implications can inform formal classroom practice.

THE STORY OF THE VIDEO PROJECT

The video project took place at Broken Hill Middle School (BHMS), a student generated pseudonym based on the name of a familiar street in the neighborhood. BHMS was a "School Under Registration Review" (SURR) in a low-income urban community in New York City (NYC). Of the approximately 1500 6th–8th graders who attended BHMS, 66% were Latino/a, 32% were African American, 1% were Asian/Pacific Islander, 0.8% were white, and 0.6% were American Indian (www. nycenet.edu). In the 2002–2003 school year, 90.4% of the BHMS student population was eligible for free lunch and had a 90.9% attendance rate. The school structured its classes around a tracking system consisting of "honors", "moderate", and "lower level" classes.

From 2001 to 2004, I worked with two groups of sixth and seventh grade students to design and produce three mini-documentaries that expressed their ideas about science in their lives: "What We Bring to Science", "Survival: What Animals and

People Need to Survive", and "The Cycle of Life". The groups named themselves Fabulous Five and Survival.

Fabulous Five

Fabulous Five was the first group to participate in the video project. The group was started by a sixth-grade boy called Star[1]. In November 2001, Star asked if he could help edit some video footage I had taken while working on a science literacy project with his class. I told Star that it sounded like a great idea and suggested that he ask some friends if they also wanted to help. Star asked four sixth grade friends, all of whom thought the project sounded fun but only two were willing to give up their lunchtime to work on the project (the students' only free time during the school day was at lunch). When asking his friends, another student in Star's class, Adel, overheard and asked Star if she could be part of the project. Star agreed and we had our first meeting on a Tuesday during the sixth grade lunch period; a fifth student, Juan, overhead the first meeting and later asked to join. Over the course of several weeks, the group stabilized at five students: Star, Mel, Juan, Janet, and Adel. Toward the end of the first year of the project, this group of students called themselves *Fabulous Five* because, "there are five of us and we are fabulous".

The members of Fabulous Five reflected the ethnic, social, economic and academic structure of the school. Two of the students were from Puerto Rico, one was from the Dominican Republic, one was a first generation American of Ghanaian descent, and one was African American. All of the students qualified for free school lunch. One of the students was in the "honors" ESL classes while the other four were in the same "lower level" classes. The five students demonstrated a range of interests in science and in academic performance.

Because Fabulous Five was the first group to participate in the project, they set up many of the ground rules used by the second group. They decided, in collaboration with me, that the movie should focus on the use of science in their everyday lives; that students should play a strong role in the video as opposed to using more official science experts like teachers and doctors; and that the movies should be filmed on site at school, in the neighborhood and around the city when possible.

Survival

Survival was the second group to participate in the video project. The group consisted of four sixth grade students from BHMS. In September of 2002, I returned to BHMS to conduct three group debriefing interviews with Fabulous Five. In one of these interviews, the members of Fabulous Five explained that they wanted to be part of making a second movie but instead of making the movie themselves they wanted to teach a new group of sixth graders how to make their own movie. Worried that there might be overwhelming interest in participation, Fabulous Five decided that the new group would be selected via the use of an application process. Each member of the Survival group was required to write a one page explanation of why she or he wanted to be part of the video project and what role they wanted to play (i.e. producer, director, music director, etc.), submit a written recommendation from a sixth grade teacher and attend an informational meeting in which Fabulous Five explained what the video project was and how it worked. Fabulous Five would then select from the people who had completed all parts of their application process. The members of Survival were the only students to complete all three parts.

Survival consisted of four sixth grade boys, Roger, Wilson, Anthony, and Rich. Within the group one student was African American and three were Puerto Rican. All group members lived in the surrounding neighborhood and were eligible for the school's free lunch program. Two of the boys were in the same "honors level" tracked classes while the other two shared the same "low level" tracked classes. Upon completion of their first mini-documentary, the four boys named their group "Survival" because their video was about how "animals use science to survive".

In September 2003, I returned to BHMS to conduct three group debriefing interviews with Survival and to determine the next steps for the video project. During the interviews, Survival expressed an interest in making a second movie and Wilson requested adding two friends from his "honors level" classes to the group. The group agreed and Mark and Tony became the final members of the video project. This group of six boys created the third and final video project mini-documentary entitled, "The Cycle of Life".

IMPROVISATIONAL ACTIONS AND THE VIDEO PROJECT

Agency is both a dynamic and generative process deeply connected to the context in which an activity takes place and who the students are or want to be at that moment (i.e. identity). In the context of the video project, students engaged in "improvisational actions" in order to transform and expand their figured worlds. Improvisational actions are recognized as moments when individuals or the group used their resources creatively to change the norms or routines of the project thus altering their figured worlds. As students made changes in their figured worlds, they also shifted perception of themselves as science learners.

The ill-structured nature of the science video project created numerous opportunities for the students to negotiate their participation with the instructors and their peers. Each of the students involved negotiated their participation in the project on both group and individual levels. For example, as a group, Survival strategically planned their participation in the negotiation of their movie themes. The goal of the Survival members was to create a project that would require fieldtrips. When the floor was opened to discuss the theme of their first movie, the students only suggested themes that would require them leaving the school grounds in order to collect the appropriate footage. The result was the selection of the theme "Survival: What Animals and People Need to Survive". Selecting this theme "required" the students to take a field trip to the zoo during the school day and take multiple walking tours of their neighborhood during Technology Club.

Similarly, at the beginning of Fabulous Five's video production process each of the members had determined that they wanted their ideas and experiences to be the central focus of their movie. As such, when discussing possible themes for their movie each of the members of Fabulous Five was cautious to only propose ideas in which their lives and ideas would be the primary focus. The result was the creation of a movie that primarily featured members of Fabulous Five and took place largely outside of the school building.

On an individual level, each student negotiated their participation in the video project by purposefully selecting their video production roles (i.e. director, production manager, production assistant or music director). The students based this selection on their areas of interest, the types of technology they desired to have most available to them and the level of responsibility they wished to assume. For example, Juan elected to be the music director "because [he] like music a lot" and he thought by being music director he would be able to use the project computer to go on line and download songs. Wilson elected to be the director of his group's movie "because [he] didn't think that the people that were in [his] group were capable of taking the director [role]. So when [he] wrote that [he] wanted to be the director [he] thought [he] could lead the group to success."

A common way students initiated negotiation is through what I refer to as "strategic questions" as questions that are intended to achieve a desired physical/material outcome. Strategic questions are those that focus on altering the student's existing figured world, whether or not the question is specifically science related. Had Star never asked if he could help me edit video footage of class presentations connected to another project, I would not have included students in the editing process and the Technology Club would not have existed. To understand the full strategy of the question, it is important to recognize that before Star introduced the topic, video editing had never been discussed. Before he asked to help edit the footage I had not even planned on editing it. Star asked to help edit the footage because his older brother had just taken a video production class at his high school. Star thought the technology his brother was able to use as part of the class was "cool" and he wanted to create a similar opportunity for himself.

In each of the production processes, it was the students' strategic questions that framed their participation in the video project. For example, Survival believed that meeting for one hour once a week was not enough time to accomplish their video production goals. In an effort to alleviate this problem, the members of Survival often asked if they could meet after school on other days, over weekends and/or over school vacations. While this question was not always met with the desired response from the instructors, the intent of the question served different purposes at various stages of the project. At the beginning of video production, the members of Survival asked for additional work time because they wanted more time to "play" with video cameras and computers. Toward the end of video production, the same students asked for more work time in order to create a video that was closest to the one they had envisioned making.

The students in Fabulous Five and Survival used strategic action to negotiate their participation in an effort to create an environment that they thought would be "fun" for them by convincing their friends to join the project. Star convinced his friend Mel to be part of the production crew and Adel put a lot of effort in recruiting her friend Janet. Similarly, when deciding whether or not to apply to be one of the members of the second video production crew, Anthony convinced three of his friends to apply with him in the hopes that one or all would take part in the project with him.

IMPROVISATIONAL ACTIONS AND EXPANDING WORLDS

When Tara came inside my class and talked to us about the video project I became interested, and I wanted to enter it because I love science. So I came down to the science lab (Wilson, Grade 7, 2002).

As indicated in the transcript above, Wilson joined the video project because he loved science. However, due to a strong focus on literacy and math test score, students at BHMS took part in 14 literacy and 12 math periods a week while only getting two to three science periods and the majority of school sanctioned after school programs revolved around literacy and math test preparation. Wilson took part in the video project because he wanted opportunities to engage his love of science. I begin with this quote because it provides a glimpse into how students sought to transform their worlds through the video project. In this section, I explain three main goals of the students' improvisational actions: (1) gaining access to technology; (2) exploring science in and outside of their community; and (3) having fun.

Gaining Access to Technology

Like many middle school students, the students of the video project had a strong understanding of technology and a deep desire for the opportunities to use it. However, of the eleven students in the Technology Club, only four had a working computer at home and only two students had ever operated a video camera. The students negotiated the framework for the video project such that, over time, participation would allow for relatively unlimited access to computers, editing equipment and video cameras. This access to technology was important to the students for two reasons. First, it was a visible change to their figured worlds. Before the video project, the students' worlds were often marked by limited or no access to computer equipment in school. After the first meeting of each production crew, the students had markedly more access as they had computers and video cameras available for their continued use. Second, as the students started to recognize the access that they had gained, they began seeking other types of access by changing their questions and expanding their ideas. For example, at the beginning of Fabulous Five's video production process, the students were content collecting video footage within the school. They filmed their teachers in the hallways, some after school classes and attempted a virtual school tour. As the students became comfortable with the video camera, they asked if they could film the school from the outside. Then they asked if they could film the neighborhood around the school and later the neighborhoods around their homes.

As the students gained greater access to the technology in the video project, they began to recognize it as part of their video production lives. The use of the computers, video cameras and editing equipment became the students' regular expectations.

The norm in their lives changed. As the norms changed so did the students' expectations of the Technology Club instructors and of themselves. The students began to expect more freedom with respect to the use of the equipment. Technology use became less important than using the technology well and creating a product they were proud of. Access to resources afforded expanded agency, which, expanded the scope and expectations of the students' questions. This, in turn, offered the students access to new and different resources, identities and figured worlds.

Gaining Access to Science In and Outside of their Neighborhood

After Survival's first production meeting it was clear that one of the group's main goals was to use the video project as a vehicle for taking science related fieldtrips in and around NYC. Specifically, the students wanted to go to the Bronx Zoo and the NYC Aquarium.

As a result, during the discussion of the themes, members of Survival clearly explained why a visit to the zoo and/or aquarium would be required to fully cover suggested topics such as "the life of fish", "interactions of humans with nature" and "interaction between animals". As part of their explanations, they offered scientifically based reasons for how a trip to the zoo would advance the research for their movie. For example, when explaining his ideas for "the life of fish", Rich stated, "to make a good movie we will need more than goldfish, like sharks and stingrays and stuff and we should get them in their natural environments. We can go to the aquarium to film that". With this statement Rich clearly presented the need for the Survival members to visit the aquarium and alluded to the idea that without going to the aquarium they would be unable to make a "good movie". Wilson supported Rich's argument by commenting that if Survival was going to talk about what "lots of types of animals need to survive we need to collect information about lots of different species".

What is important about this example is that students used the topic of animal exploration to validate their need to go on fieldtrips. This is one example of how the students used science and their knowledge of particular subject matter (i.e., categorization of animals and taxonomy) to justify their choices. In this way, the students' use of strategy was more sophisticated than simply using the video project to go outside. They used the construct of science and science content as supporting tools to justify why they "*needed*" to go to on trips. In order to support their science learning on these trips, the students arranged interviews with multiple zookeepers and aquarium guides and researched information on particular animals prior to each trip. In this way, the students were forced to think more deeply about what science is, what counted as science, and in what ways scientific content could be applied to achieve a specific goal (i.e., taking a fieldtrip). Thus, the students showed themselves to be critically aware of both science and the environment of the video project and had the ability to strategically use their critical awareness to alter their figured worlds.

Similarly, when Fabulous Five finalized the theme for their movie, they actively selected a theme that would allow them to collect video footage outside of the school.

During a movie theme discussion, Adel proposed that the group make a movie explaining the science they have learned in school but from their perspective. At first the rest of the group was not very excited about the idea. Mel then suggested that if the group followed Adel's idea they could interview each other and their classmates. Though this did raise the excitement level of the group, they were not yet sold. Then Star suggested that they could make a movie explaining the science they learn in school and showing the same science outside of school. Juan then added that if they were going to make a movie about science outside of school, then they would "have to" film outside of school. Thus, similar to Survival, Fabulous Five used science to gain access to the outdoors. While the students could have used interviews to explain the relationship between school science and the science "happening outside of school", when the students realized that they could gain access to filming outside they argued that it would be "more scientific" to film the science happening outside rather than to just talk about it.

Having Fun

One of the primary reasons each of the students gave for taking part in the video project was because they thought it would be "fun". When pressed to define what they thought would be "fun" about being part of the Technology Club, the students cited being able to "play with the video camera", "work with their friends", "hangout in the science lab" and "going on trips". "Fun" is partly about choices: choices to socially align with whom they want, to select topics that they care about, and to investigate those topics in ways that they think are worthwhile.

As illustrated by the examples below, what made the project "fun" for the students existed on both a physical and emotional level. In order to create an environment that they recognized as fun, students drew on multiple resources. They encouraged friends to join the project. They negotiated their participation in ways that gave them access to unique privileges (i.e., leaving the school grounds during the school day). They negotiated for more time to use the technology and they created space to make their work visible to their teachers and peers (i.e., electing to show their movies at the sixth grade end of year assemblies).

The emotional aspect of what made the video project fun for the students was linked to their use of negotiation and availability of resources. At its core, this feeling of fun is based in the students' belief that, within the space of the video project, they were trusted and their ideas, choices, wants and needs were important and valued. For most participants, this was the most dramatic alteration to their school figured worlds.

In a post-production interview, Star explained this concept:

Tara: So why do you think making a movie about science would be fun?
Star: I don't know, it was just fun to do. It was fun to learn about ourselves and stuff.
Tara: When you were part of the project, was it always fun?
Star: It was fun. We had our bad days and our good days. We had our separations; people wanted to drop out and then come back in like

> Mel and Janet. They dropped out and came back and nobody wanted to do anything when they left us by ourselves. We were like Oh my God but it was cool. It was fun - us learning about ourselves and making a video to let people understand.

Tara: Understand what?

Star: Science better - the younger kids.

Tara: So looking back on it now, are you glad you did it? If so, why?

Star: Yeah, because it was fun. It was a different experience than a regular project. We had science and the real world out there and we had to put it together. *We looked at anything and then we had to relate it to science.* You never see a teacher do a project like that. They don't assign projects like that.

Tara: Before you said what made it so different from something you've done in class is really the technology you got to use. S o now you're saying it's something more than that?

Star: It was everything. You can't say it was one thing and not the other. It was the whole experience. It was everything, the technology, the searching, everything. It was just different. Because teachers just be like search the computer. We had to look out there and put it with what we were studying.

It is clear from the interview above that Star believes he took part in something special. Although Star tries to explain what specifically about the video project was so "fun" for him, in the end he says he cannot find "one thing" to explain it. What made this project "fun" to Star is that it was a special project, unlike anything he had done before. It was a project that asked for his authentic input and required that he and his group members search for solutions rather than being given the answers.

In his video project application essay, Anthony wrote: "I really want to be the director of photography because I really enjoy taking pictures of nature. I'm really good at it. I even got a camera". He thought the video project would be fun because it would allow for him to take part in an activity he liked (namely taking pictures of nature), had experience with, and felt confident in doing. In a group debriefing interview, Rich said that he took part in the project because he "thought it would be fun to get to choose things to film."

WHY IMPROVISING WORLDS MATTERS

During their involvement in the video project, the students began to express themselves and their participation in science in positive and empowering ways (i.e., as people who knew science and believed that their ideas were interesting and valuable). Anthony, for example, initially took part in the project because he "thought it would be fun to film stuff" and he "really enjoy[ed] taking pictures of nature." However, due to his history of failing grades and negative interactions with his science teachers, at the beginning of his participation Anthony could not conceive that he would ever understand enough science or be allowed to participate long enough in order to complete a movie. As Anthony began to see his ideas put to use in the production of Survival's movie, he started to recognize that the members of Survival and the Technology Club instructors valued his ideas and supported his participation. With this realization, Anthony's desire to be involved in the video project shifted from wanting time and space to play with the video camera to re-presenting himself to his teachers and peers as a person who "can accomplish". When asked what he enjoyed about the video project, Anthony replied "I like that I accomplished it and it showed people I can accomplish something hard". Anthony's science teachers described him as "lower achieving" and "generally disruptive". Anthony used the video project to re-invent himself.

Though over the course of his participation Anthony was often reminded to not interrupt others when they were speaking, the more he felt his input was welcomed rather than silenced, the more comfortable he became with listening to and using others' ideas. This is particularly powerful because once Anthony was able to see his ideas combined with the ideas of his production crew, he developed a new understanding of what he could accomplish. With this new understanding came the want and need to re-identify himself to those who only knew the "bad kid". In an effort to change his school and science identities, during the production process Anthony often requested to be interviewed as the expert on particular science topics and if he was not the expert, he asked the group if he could conduct the interview. On numerous occasions, Anthony asked Mr. H (his sixth grade math teacher and a Technology Club instructor) if he told other teachers about how hard he (Anthony) worked in the Technology Club.

All of the students of the video project have a story similar to Anthony. For some, like Adel, they always believed they were capable of great work but felt they never had space to show just how smart they were. For others, like Juan and Roger, who started the project rarely speaking a word and by the end frequently offered me unsolicited critical feedback for improvement, the video project provided a safe space for their voices to be heard and, in so doing, validated that what they had to say was interesting and important. In some way or other, each of the students developed a need to show their peers, teachers and others who viewed their work that they were accomplished science authorities.

From the students' perspectives, there was a clear hierarchical order of teaching and learning at BHMS: teachers teach students and students can teach others younger than themselves. When Fabulous Five initially described the purpose of their movie, Mel explained:

> We are making this so we could be able to teach younger students what we have learned with our teachers. Just like the eighth graders get science so, they could probably make a video so they could show it to younger students like we're doing. So we could show it to the fifth graders, fourth graders, and the third graders.

As students re-identified themselves as accomplished science authorities, conflict arose between the students' new identities and the role they were expected to play in their school. This conflict resulted in students questioning and challenging the hierarchical structure that claimed students could not teach their teachers and older students could not learn from those younger than them. As stated by Star:

> We wanted to be professionals. We wanted to make a movie where people would be like wow... From my point of view, I guess we wanted to show what we were made of. To show other people that even though that we were young or despite whatever grade we were in that we're still smart and we were capable of doing whatever they did. If they did it we could do too, **we're not less than them**.

Despite the differences in each of the groups' movies, in terms of movie style, information they wanted to express and how they expressed that information, the fundamental ideas about how science content should be expressed had a singular origin. Both groups began the process believing that the best way of explaining the science in their movie was to find "qualified" adults to explain the science content. For Fabulous Five, this meant collecting footage of their science teacher teaching science class. For Survival, this meant interviewing professional "science people" such as doctors, veterinarians, zoologists, and their science teacher. As the production process progressed, however, both Fabulous Five and Survival discovered that they wanted to paint a different picture of what science was and how it related to their lives.

By the time Fabulous Five had completed their mini-documentary, they had cut all footage from inside the science classroom and most of the footage from within the school building itself arguing, "Science is everything and all around us". This new view of science opened the door to the idea that science could take place in their neighborhood and in other spaces outside the originally understood structure of science (i.e. the science classroom, hospitals and laboratories). This realization caused the students to challenge who they perceived as knowing and doing science. The students recognized that science took place in the science classroom because the teachers knew science. Science took place in hospitals because doctors knew science. However, they did not recognize teachers or doctors (the traditional people who know science) as being part of their neighborhood. As such, they were forced to question who knew the science in their neighborhood to allow science to be practiced there. After months of group conversations and investigating what "counted" as science, the students of Fabulous Five decided that "everyone knows science" including themselves, their peers and their families.

The belief that everyone knows science evolved into a situation in which the members of Fabulous Five became the authorities of the science information rather than accepting teachers or doctors as the authorities. Thus after several months, when selecting people to interview in their movie they actively avoided all traditional science authorities. The result was the creation of a movie that focused on Fabulous Five teaching "others" (their peers, teachers and those younger and older then themselves) about the science in their lives. As stated by Adel in the opening of Fabulous Five's movie:

> The main focus of this video is to make people that do not know, people that know very little, very little about science, for them to understand. Instead of

giving them the science text book, which would take years for them to finally understand it, we are taking the textbook, breaking it down into pieces for them and then when they see our video they will understand it easier.

Though on a different timetable, members of Survival also came to the conclusion that they did not have to yield the authority of science teaching exclusively to science professionals. When the members of Survival were asked what they would change about their movie, Rich replied, "less interviews with adults and more footage of us talking about and doing science". Anthony quickly agreed with this comment adding, "Yeah, the doctor and vet were boring. Look [at the movie] I'm almost asleep listening to the doctor."

This shift in belief of who knows science and who is qualified to teach science was powerful for the students as it expanded the ways in which they felt they could participate in science. When asked what she felt she gained from making the mini-documentary, Janet replied, "self-confidence." She explained that she felt less shy by the end of her involvement in the video project. She felt that she knew more about science than she had once given herself credit for. An example she gave was that before doing the project, she would not have stood in front of her whole class to show her work and now she felt like "doing that again could be fun".

Star demonstrated a shift in his understanding of how he could participate in science when, in the Fabulous Five movie, he explained that his favorite type of science was exploring science. This was his favorite because, "Exploring science is like you get to know more about the world. You know, if you don't explore, what you gonna know. You expect to learn by someone else teaching you? You can learn to by you figuring it out yourself. When it comes to science, its like I'm learning about myself."

Star's understanding of his participation in science shifted from being a subject that is passively learned in a classroom to science being about exploring and in that exploration, learning about one's self. This understanding of science as exploration leads to independence: viewing science learning as a process of exploration makes it possible for Star to "explore" his own interests and not simply rely on what others teach him.

FROM AFTER SCHOOL TO IN SCHOOL

Much of the literature around informal science learning argues that students are more engaged and enthusiastic about their learning in informal learning environments because the nature of such environments is to provide students "free choice" (Roth & Calabrese Barton, 2004; Rahm, 2001; Calabrese Barton, 1998). While I believe this to be true, it is also important to understand why students make the choices they do when given "free choice". Understanding how and when students enact their agency furthers our understanding why and how students make the choices they do in informal and formal learning environments.

Within the context of the video project, the students' exertion of agency in their figured worlds not only changed the "physical environment" in which they learned science (i.e., going to the zoo, gaining access to technology) but also expanded their access and use of social and human capital. In their videos, both groups moved between school-based knowledge, as presented in school form (i.e., science text books) and formal science discourse (i.e., use of sanctioned science vocabulary), and home-based knowledge, as presented in non-school ways (i.e., storytelling and neighborhood imagery) with non-sanctioned discourse (i.e., use of slang). They also moved between symbolic capital of their peer groups and community (i.e., music selection, neighborhood landmarks) and symbolic capital of school (i.e., particular discursive practices, topic selection). Lastly, the students moved between formal assigned tasks within the school-based activity (i.e., creating a story board, selecting content focus, researching content ideas) and non school-based tasks integral to the success of their videos (i.e., getting "out of school" to capture video footage, establishing playful relationships between peer groups). Each of these fluid moves positioned the students' narrative authority in parallel planes with the epistemic authority of school.

This chapter reveals that a student's enactment of agency depends upon both the student and the context in which that student is working. At the personal level, each student has their own set of lived experiences and cultural beliefs that have developed their individual identities. As such, the aspects of an experience that encourages students to express their agency will differ based on what an individual knows or believes about themselves, about science, and/or about the context in which they are working. However, in the context of the video project, agency is expressed via the interactions with and among other individuals. For example, the students of Survival outwardly expressed their agency to the instructors of the Technology Club when they unanimously agreed to only suggest movie themes that would require taking fieldtrips. Thus, the context in which agency is expressed is critical. If, as the lead instructor of the Technology Club, I had rejected each of Survival's theme proposals arguing that we could not visit the zoo or the aquarium for any number of reasons, they may have been more reluctant to negotiate later wants and needs. However, because of the dynamic nature of agency, while the interaction described above could have left the students feeling as though their ideas and/or needs were not valued, an interaction moments or days later could shift this perspective. The point being that while students will outwardly express their agency in environments where they know it will be supported, supporting a student's expression of agency does not mean doing exactly what they want all of the time.

The relationship between the individual and the social context is important for two reasons. First, students' expression of agency is based on the students' current understanding of their figured worlds. This understanding is based on the students' beliefs about themselves and their beliefs of what others think of them. Students express agency to make positive changes to their figured worlds. Thus, agency is a tool students use to effect change at both the personal and social level. Second, how much students are able to expand their agency is framed by the social context in which the agency is expressed.

In reference to this notion of the expansion of agency being contingent on the social context, it is important to note that most of the students in the video project were placed in the "low level" classes at their school largely because their grades and standardized test scores were low. What I find most interesting is that these same students, who have received low school grades and test scores, demonstrated "honors level" skills within the context of the video project. They used an extra-ordinary set of strategies for learning new science and technology, demonstrated an insatiable desire to learn science content and a remarkable ability to incorporate new ideas and constructs into their ways of knowing. Anthony is an example of one such student.

When I explained to Anthony's science teacher that I wanted to observe him in class because he was part of the video project, she was astonished. Her astonishment over Anthony's participation existed on two levels. First, why would a student who "clearly does not want to learn" want to be part of a project that made movies about science? Secondly, how could I possibly think Anthony would be anything other than the problem child he was in her class? While it is true that Anthony was one of the most challenging students to take part in the project, as he came to believe that his ideas and needs were valued and that he had knowledge to contribute (primarily about reptiles), there was marked improvement in his behavior, in his ability to listen to others' ideas and in his desire to learn new science content. Anthony in the Technology Club was not the same Anthony I observed in the science classroom. For example, during Technology Club Anthony asked questions and researched science content in an effort to position himself as a vital member of Survival. In his science classroom, Anthony asked questions and made comments in an effort to make people laugh and often to cover-up that he did not know the science content being discussed. When asked during a production meeting why he did not take as much interest in information taught in his science class as he did in the information he had taught himself about reptiles during the video project, Anthony replied, "what's the point?" In the figured world of his science class Anthony understood that he was a "bad kid" who "doesn't like science" and "can't learn science". In his figured world of the Technology Club Anthony was "a reptile expert" and someone who could "accomplish something hard". Within the video project students were able to alter their science figured worlds because the learning context was open to student feedback, responsive to student voice and assisted students in determining their own strategies to meet the expectations of their instructors and their production crew (i.e., supported student agency).

NOTES

[1] Pseudonym selected by the student because he was "gonna be a star". All other names are pseudonyms assigned by the author.

HAYAT ALHOYOKEM, ANGELA CALABRESE BARTON
AND EDNA TAN

4. PARTICIPATING IN AND TRANSFORMING COMMUNITIES OF PRACTICE

California strawberries are far, far away
Michigan Strawberries are really close today
Using a truck to get them here
Will cause pollution
There is a solution
The solution is to pick strawberries here
They don't have to go far when they are near
Energy is money
And money is time
When we drive down the street
We are on a very fine line
To save the earth
And have our berries
Buy them local
Do not tarry
Word.
    —*Rap produced spontaneously by Shawna & Cathy during a unit on the 100-mile diet, July 2008. To listen to the rap, go to: http://barton.wiki.educ.msu.edu/file/view/strawberry_rapfinal.m4a*

Kathy and Shawna, authors of the rap above, were two of several youth at an urban community club who were involved in a summer program focused on investigating the "farm to table systems" in the US. Both 11-year-old girls were adamant on engaging in this environmental issue in relation with their real lives, particularly in relation with the food they eat. When deciding upon a way to express their views about food transportation, they chose to create a rap about strawberries because they thought it would be a good way to compare the differences between local and imported strawberries. Strawberries were also one of the main products that they had tasted earlier in the unit. They had compared the taste of strawberry pop-tarts, frozen strawberries, strawberry jam and fresh strawberries as part of looking at the broader picture of food packaging, processing and transportation. So, before making the rap they had engaged in several activities and discussions regarding "what happens to food from farm to table" and how that affects the environment.

*S.J. Basu et al., (eds.), Democratic Science Teaching: Building the Expertise to Empower
Low-Income Minority Youth in Science, 55–73.*

As a transition activity between exploring the main components of the current farming system (food production, processing and packaging, and transportation) and further investigating how each of these aspects contributed to carbon emissions and a carbon footprint, students were asked to create posters that "mapped out" what they thought was the farm to store process, using the example of a strawberry one might purchase in a mid-Michigan store. Students were encouraged to use the computers to find images and additional information to augment their posters. As Kathy's group planned out their poster they began to write a rap song that explained the problems associated with the current farm to store system. In addition to using the computers to look for pictures, they opened up Garageband, a Mac program that is designed for amateurs to compose their own musical pieces. Garageband allows users to choose among a variety of musical instruments and sound effects that they could play using an on screen keyboard. The girls and their group mates enjoyed this feature and began to play around with beats to liven up their song. They even stayed after the session is over that day to get their rap recorded because they thought that their rap did a better job explaining the farm to store system than did their poster. After trying several beats for their rap on Garageband, Shawna gave up and decided to drum out the beats herself on the table instead for the sound effects.

Episodes like the one presented above raise questions about how students leverage their narrative experiences towards becoming what we have referred to elsewhere as "community science experts" (Calabrese Barton & Tan, 2010). In other words, how do students use their own positions – their cultural knowledge and experiences – to gain a voice in both science and their communities? We are also interested especially in the ways in which youth construct hybrid discourses, or discourses that call upon the ways of knowing and being and the specialized language of both the peer community and of science to do. We wonder not only "when" do youth take up such hybrid discourses, but also what are their forms, and what role(s) do they play in (re)positioning the youth as community science experts. Finally, we wonder, what does this all teach us about democratic and empowering science classrooms?

In this chapter we take up these questions in the context of a summer science program focused on engaging youth in a critical exploration of the 100 mile diet. The 100 mile diet is a concept that challenges one to examine the impact that the globalization of the typical diet has on environmental health and sustainability, the local economy, and the broader food system. Drawing upon classroom footage, student interviews and student work and critical discourse analysis we examined how teachers and students "talked" to each other through student work and class-room dialog, and how that talk changed over time, noting how the language students used positioned themselves and others with particular roles and expertise.

BECOMING AN EXPERT: MEANINGFUL PARTICIPATION AND DISCOURSE

All learning and activity is situated historically, culturally and socially (Rogoff, 2003). How or why youth make sense of their worlds depends, in part, on the cultural practices of their families and communities, and what counts as meaningful knowledge are closely tied to their families and communities values (Rogoff, 2003). Yet, the kind of learning that happens in science learning communities tends to focus on "final form" science with little attention to the cultural practices which give rise to that science. Learning tends to be "about" practice rather than learning practice itself. Teachers, curriculum developers, and school systems tend to treat students as "objects" of the process, rather than youth in the process.

When participation becomes the focal point in learning as opposed to, for example, final form science, a critical eye can be placed on how communities mediate the process of coming to know and coming to be. We are inspired by Lave and Wenger's (1991) work on "legitimate peripheral participation," for this calls attention to how participation in a community of practice rests on the contradictions of production and reproduction. For example, while the community is producing new artifacts, the newcomer brings new resources and tools and engages in the process of re-producing artifacts as well as producing innovative ones. As newcomers are exposed to and appropriate the tools, discourses, and practices of a community they also, at the same time, leverage their cultural knowledge and experience from outside of that community, transforming, or producing new legitimate versions of participation and expertise. Therefore we believe we must be mindful of how power mediates the process of enculturation into new communities of practice.

Participating in the "Discourse" of a Community

One of the most poignant ways to understand how "learning to participate" in a community of practice is as much political as it cultural and cognitive, is to turn to Discourse[1]. Discourses – because they reflect systems of knowing, doing, thinking, writing and expressing oneself in a social setting – influence how one approaches a new community and the kinds of conversations and experiences he or she is willing to engage in and learn from. Often the dominant Discourse of traditional science talk is laden with the authority of science, placing students not familiar with this Discourse in marginal positions. Lemke (1990. p. 172) points out that "[t]he language of science is not part of students' native language. It is a foreign "register" (specialized subset of a language) within English, and it sounds foreign and uncomfortable to most students until they have practiced using it for a long time." This means students' different Discourses are often at odds with the traditional science Discourses of books and teachers.

While vast differences can exist in the Discourses that youth bring to school and the Discourse of science, not all researchers frame these differences as unbridgeable. For example, Calabrese Barton and Tan (2009) identify the various funds of knowledge and Discourses that students bring with them to classroom in a low income urban school. Their study shows how teachers, with explicit attention to Discourse, can adapt instructional approaches to legitimize the family funds, community funds, peer culture and popular culture funds which are the knowledge funds from which various Discourse emerge, as meaningful and appropriate tools in science learning. Such an approach to how Discourses converge is important in opening up dialogue and practice on how to bridge a students' movement to the Dominant discourse of

57

science without being alienated from someone's original or primary discourse. Many of the students in the study felt "authorized" to engage in a topic in a non-traditional setting and take initiative when necessary. For example one student who was considered a "trouble maker" shifted his position to one who leads a group investigating fruits and argued the value of nutrition to price in addition to offering fruit snacks to the rest of the classmates. This was a situation when engaging with a topic that leverages of family and popular cultural funds positioned the students in an expert position that allowed him "to participate with authority in science" as the authors mentioned. This means that providing such opportunities for the youth is important to blend the primary discourse with the secondary Discourse.

Transformative Hybridity

Recent work on Discourse and science learning has focused on how to scaffold students in appropriating the Discourses of science that are accepted within the practice community. Reveles, Cordora and Kelly (2004), for example, foreground the role of the teacher, in situating "literacy in the collective actions of the community of learners and [making] connections to the disciplinary practices of science" (p. 1140). In their study with elementary science students, the teacher utilized a "co-constructive" (p. 1140) pedagogical approach by specifically acknowledging inherent student identities that were brought into the science classroom. In the classroom Discourse, students' personal experiences with the subject matter were explicitly encouraged by the teacher and leveraged upon to delve deeper into the science content at hand. In this manner, deliberate connections were made between school science and the relevant community knowledge students bring with them into the classroom. Through the careful attention paid toward managing scientific discourse in an inclusive manner and the enactment of inquiry-based lessons, the elementary students in the study formulated positive academic identities and could see themselves acting as scientists. Towards the end of the study, the "students were speaking, explaining, arguing and personifying the action of scientists who were capable and literate regarding knowledge and understanding about science" (p. 1140). Students were able to articulate what it is that they do that allow them to see themselves as scientists, thus "formulating their identities as students, acting as scientists" (p. 1142).

As Reveles and his colleagues point out, in order to engage students in a meaningful discourse, it is important to have a teacher who can blend various discourses the students are accustomed to with the academic discourse, that is create a hybrid discourse that is safe enough for all students to participate and rich enough in order to push on learning the required academic content. However, this process of working towards hybrid Discourses is often fraught with issues of power, for the science practices one learns to engage in do not always validate the cultural resources that learners bring to the process.

Hybrid Discourses have taken on several different meanings in the research literature in education (Moje, 2004). The dominant use of hybridity is in explaining how the gap between primary discourses and the Dominant Discourse of the classroom can be bridged. This approach to hybridity is often discussed through terms such as becoming bilingual or code switching, focusing on opportunities to help individuals engage in the Dominant Discourse while maintaining someone's original primary discourse. The second use is to draw from different funds of knowledges and everyday discourses in order to succeed in various discourses. Take, for example, Sharma's (2007) efforts to describe how students in an Indian village exercise agency in order to bring their own everyday discourse and knowledge source about electricity to the classroom. This everyday discourse of students when blended with the classroom discourse has helped the students in learning the academic science discourse. The classroom then was a laboratory in which a hybrid discourse was exercised and the teacher acting as what Sharma (2008) calls "bricoleur" successfully draws on students' discourses and merges it with the intended scientific discourse. The third use of discourse is one which highlights some-one's position in the environment as an empowered individual who is participating actively in the community to learn a certain practice but also to influence or transform that practice by reshaping it. This is the concept that we adopt in describing our work here. It is this latter form of hybridity we see in the rap presented at the beginning of this chapter. Kathy and Shawna created the rap as a supplement to their poster, and in their words, a "better" explanation of the farm to store system. Their description of the system was replete with scientific ideas but was positioned as relevant and meaningful to their lives at that moment, in both its form and function. Using rhythm/cadence, word choice, and adding socioeconomic and political undertones to their explanation of a highly complex system (i.e., energy is money and money is time), they not only exerted an expertise relevant to their local learning community, they also positioned themselves in such a way to influence the community of practice around them.

The above discussion, therefore, points out that learning is not a static cognitive concept that is reserved only to the selected "smart" ones but is a social dynamic concept that happens through participation of the individual in meaningful hybrid discourses. One importance of a hybrid discourse is bridging the gap among various discourses and positioning individuals in an active location to influence the commu-nity. However, it is also important to help us understanding the repertoire for participating in a certain practice such as understanding how and why certain pattern of behavior or thought is exhibited among a certain group. Understanding those repertoires is important to help us move away from stereotyping individuals. Gutierrez and Rogoff (2003) further remind us of the unjust fixed labeling of individuals when they warn us against the possibility of being able to "nail down" the stable characteristics or regularities of certain cultural groups especially non-dominant ones which in turn leads to "prescriptive" teaching methods. Fixing individuals into traits deprives learning from its dynamic property and enhances stereotypes which is what happens when one classifies certain groups with the trait of holistic learner or that of analytic learners. The result is a certain prescribed method for each group which neglects the "history of engagement" of an individual in a certain practice. Rather, it is important to conceive of a "repertoire for participating in practice" that could identify the artifacts, context and background the individuals carry with them. For example, understanding the dynamic intricacies of the "repertoires" individuals or groups bring with them to the table is the first step towards thinking about how individuals learn. A hybrid Discourse opens the floor for the primary discourse that one acquires from the original cultural practice to be exposed and appreciated. The "repertoire of practice" then becomes a useful tool for classroom Discourse and this hybrid discourse is a way to unpack this "repertoire of practice" and transform into an active practice outside the original community of practice.

We therefore perceive a hybrid discourse as one way that could help in legitimate peripheral participation and the same time push the community in different directions. Having both concepts of "legitimate peripheral participation" and "transformative hybridity" as main ideas that guide learning, we examine the effect of such partici-pation and practice on youth participation in constructing knowledge about their food and environment. We think that by opening the floor for a "hybrid discourse" when dealing with "non-traditional" science topic in a "non-traditional" educational setting (club rather school), we attempted to help youth participating in the program engage in a legitimate participation of those issues.

LEARNING TO PARTICIPATE IN GREEN ENERGY TECHNOLOGIES

Green Energy Technologies in the City: GET City

The club where we worked with the youth is an urban community-based club, where the youth of different ages join the club any time they wish from 8 am to 5 pm. There are many activities that the youth can do in the club (sports, crafts, playing games, etc). Note that all the activities (with the exception of GET City) that the club offered were non-academic in nature For the youth, the club is a place where they have close friends they can play, laugh, eat, talk and spar with. From our experience in the club, we noticed that most of the youth know each other and there are close ties that allow various individuals to take care of each other and support each other. The club contained several rooms each room serving a specific purpose. For example there was a room where computer games were found and some of youth were often playing games on the computer. In that same room there was a billiard table where some peers were often seen playing. Another room was an indoor basketball court and was used as conference room when major announce-ments for all club members needed to happen. Every day between 12:30 and 1 pm, all club member youth had lunch together in the lunch room. The lunch room was a large hall with many long tables and chairs. After lunch, all the tables were cleared and cleaned and we were able to use this room after lunch three times a week for the GET city program.

The GET City program is a program introduces science as a Discourse that is intertwined with other kinds of Discourse while investigating green energy-related concerns. GET City had a good reputation among club members and we had several requests from younger students who felt that they wanted to join the program and the various activities involved. Particularly the use of technology such as having individual internet access was very important to youth. Each participant had his or her laptop and could surf the internet for information and use excel and i-movie features which helped express their ideas more efficiently.

Studying Carbon Footprints

During the summer of 2008, we concentrated on "linking the food to the environment" and used the concept of "eating locally" as an overarching theme through which we addressed scientific and non-scientific issues such as the carbon foot print, how to calculate one's carbon footprint, in gaining a deeper understanding of the influence that one's individual choices and behavior have on the global environment. We ran 3 sessions per week for five weeks and each session lasted for 2 hours, with two extra work sessions for those who desired the extra time. The youth in this program were 15 members of 11 and 12 years of age, most of them were regular attendants and few missed sessions. In the unit, we used the concept of a carbon footprint as the main learning goal or big idea through which we related investigations of food choices and habits. Our main learning objectives, from a science standpoint, included: calculating distances on maps and transforming that to real distances, defining the carbon footprint concept and identifying factors the contribute to increasing or decreasing the carbon footprint of food, using the excel program to create comparative representations (line or bar graphs, pie charts) that could compare the carbon footprint of different foods and constructing scientific arguments about the carbon footprint of food.

We planned the unit in three phases: Exploring the food system; Linking the Food System to Carbon Emissions; and Investigating the local Food System of the lunch and the Canteen.

The *first phase* (Exploring food system) focused on developing awareness of one's own eating practices and its relationship to their personal carbon footprint. Lessons included completing and then discussing a carbon footprint calculation, taste testing similar foods of different global origins and levels of packaging, and mapping distances traveled using GIS software. We had a double goal for this section: the first was to engaged participants in some interesting fun activities of tasting a variety of food (for example local strawberries and imported strawberries) and giving their opinion about them, and the second was to have them think about the different foods that they eat from an environmental perspective. After they filled out an activity about which food they tasted better, we gave the participants maps where they had to measure the distances on the map where each food came from by a ruler and make the calculations of the actual distance. This gave them a concrete sense of how far the food has to travel in order to reach them. This idea of distance was further reinforced when they used GIS to locate where the food was and find out the distance the food items traveled using the software as well.

The *second phase* (Linking the Food System to Carbon Emissions) involved delving into the idea of the carbon foot print and comparing the different aspects of food like packaging processing and transportation. We first started by concentrating on the story of strawberries where the participants split into groups depending on what they liked to do. Distance was one aspect that he participants focused on and comparing strawberries in different forms was another aspect. Participants thought hard of the distance strawberry travelled and its relation to carbon footprint and compared different strawberry products in terms of the distance they travelled. They also were given strawberry in different forms (fresh strawberry, strawberry jam, poptarts, etc...) and they had compared the carbon footprint for those. One group made the rap discussed earlier that talked about local and imported strawberry and used this song in the final project. A second group prepared a PowerPoint presentation about the various information they have learnt concerning local and non-local food, and a third group prepared a poster that illustrated the comparison between local and imported strawberries by drawing, coloring and writing comments. After this, we prepared more internet based activities and class discussions about the carbon foot print and its relation to what we eat. For example, in one session we discussed a new article about milk jugs and its shape in relation to its trans-portation. This activity was based on a new article in New York Times and a documentary on YouTube and the participants found that interesting and engaging. Using excel program the participants also worked on comparing food energy in corn to various energy expended in the production, distribution, processing, packaging, of corn products. Students discussed these issues among their groups. This second phase was a bridge between the first and third phases. It built on the preliminary knowledge about food aspects such as distance to move on to thinking about other aspects of food such as packaging and processing. Moreover, it helped participants gain more knowledge about carbon foot printing which was useful to have them when investigating a major part of their life in the club, eating lunch and canteen items.

The *third phase* of the program (Investigating the local Food System of the lunch and the Canteen) involved an investigation into the carbon footprint of the Club's lunch and Canteen program. Students gathered data about their own lunch and canteen products, include food production, processing and packaging, transportation and preparation for consumption. They analyzed each approach for the input of resources and the output of carbon and waste. (They were expected to gather both quantitative data such as the number of lunches served, measurement of food packing in terms of mass and volume, number of snacks consumed, number of meals thrown in the trash and so on). They were also expected to generate qualitative data, including pictorial evidence of the production of waste, interview data on peers' food practices, interviews with experts involved in different phases of the food system and so on.

During this phase, students also took field trips to an organic farm, the public school system lunch preparation facility, and a local restaurant that served regionally grown food. The purpose of these trips was to engage with experts and to further investigate how food is produced and prepared in different food systems. This activity provided students' with an alternative of how to reduce carbon footprint, for example buying food that are organically grown in the region. It was one idea they could consider when exploring the food they eat. The participants used the discourse they have engaged in for the past five weeks in order to produce their final products. This discourse included personal stories, scientific discourse they worked on, music and personal talents such as drawing skills. For example many of the songs, PowerPoint presentations, some excel graphs produced during the unit were included in the final products. The main products submitted by the youth at the end of the sixth week were four documentaries (approximate 6 to 8 minutes) by groups that presented the result of their investigation of the club's lunch and canteen. We describe in some detail one of these documentaries to provide a sense of what they entailed.

What's Cooking Y'all?

One of the three final video products created was by an all girls grouped, self named "the Candy Rappers." The girls produced a documentary that focused on five core ideas: the first was explaining the idea of a carbon footprint and why it is relevant to everyday lunch practices, the second was delving into what kids around the club know and care about with respect to the lunch program, the third was "Dissecting" the club lunch practices, including an analysis of the lunch processing and packaging, and the fourth was to investigate the practices associated with lunch waste, and the final one was offering a range of solutions to help reduce the club lunch carbon footprint.

The movie entitled, "What's Cooking Y'all" by the Candy Rappers (which can be viewed here, http://barton.wiki.educ.msu.edu/file/view/Lunch%20carbon%20foot print.mov) begins with a dance beat, and offers a scrolling definition of a carbon footprint:

A carbon foot print is a measure of the impact human activities have on the environment in terms of the amount of greenhouse gasses produced, measured in units of carbon dioxide, (Wikipedia), the larger the carbon foot print is, the large the negative impact it has on the environment, in terms of the club's lunch program, production and packaging, transportation and aftermath, all contribute the size of carbon footprint.

The music and definition cut to a black screen that asks, "What do you know about your lunch." This is followed by several short clips of middle school and elementary school aged children talking about their lunch time eating practices at the club. (A popular song plays in the background). These interviews are at once playful – highlighting laughter among the youth as they talk to each other about their lunch practices- and serious – showcasing the youth investigators as serious about the value of the other children's lunchtime experiences, as the following scene suggests:

Youth Investigator:	What did you have on your pizza?
Student:	Pepperoni, Cheese and
Youth Investigator:	Did you eat the peaches and apple juice?
Student: Yah.	My apple juice I gave to Shar
Youth Investigator:	Did you feel full?
Student:	No
Youth Investigator:	Did you like it?
Student:	No

| Youth Investigator: | Should we have this lunch again? |
| Student: | Maybe if its warm not cold |

While the youth investigators keep a central focus on what the other children like and care about, they also delved into what food actually gets eaten (or wasted) and whether the lunch satisfied their needs.

The interviews segue into the "lunch dissection." This segment of the documentary begins with a screen shot that says "Time 4 surgery" written in red against a black screen. The title transitions into two shots of five girls with plastic gloves and glasses and kitchen utensils standing over another girl who is laying on a cafeteria table with ketchup ("blood") splattered across her chest and face. This is immediately followed by a another title page labeled "Dissection... of YOUR lunch" and a series of close up images of the lunch. The voice over explains:

> We dissected the lunch to find what we could recycle and what foods were compostable. This relates to the carbon footprint because petroleum is used to make plastic packaging which reduces the fuel available for energy. Composting is better than throwing away food because you can use the compost as fertilizer to grow your own garden which reduces the fuel emission in transporting food which reduces the carbon footprint.

The dissecting of lunch section was followed by a scrolling text of items in lunch that are recyclable and a photograph of the school lunch with arrows pointing out the various plastics used, their petroleum sources, and whether they are recyclable. In background is playing the strawberry rap that we mentioned in the beginning.

The fourth section was that of "Aftermath ... dun dun dun..." and pictures of girls dissecting club trash, and counting up 17 of trash bags for the day and calculating 5 of trash bags per week, month and year. "in 3 months it is 1020 bags of trash and in one year it 4080 bags of trash. DANG!" The section then leads to the last segment that shows different models of compost boxes the club could consider and other specific recommendations to the club to reduce is carbon footprint. Each recommendation is attributed to a specific girl: "B says: make a compost bin at the club, P says: use recyclable plastic in lunch and put recycling bins around the club, S: expand garden at club growing more vegetables and using the compost." And the video ends by "Thank you for your time" with the girls' picture in the background.

CREATING HYBRID DISCOURSES

The girls' movie, as is the case with the other three movies produced, is compelling and witty. Replete with complex descriptions of carbon footprints and its relationship to lunch program practices, the movie offers a substantial look into how energy is being used and wasted at the club. The lunch dissection offers a close analysis of the materials used in the serving of food, and the lunch waste survey provides multiple days worth of evidence regarding how much waste is produced in terms of waste, materials that could have been recycled, and materials that could have been composted. The youth used scientific terminology in defining carbon footprints, in explaining the food system and the sources of pollution, in graphically explaining their evidence regarding waste production, and in offering a set of realistic recommendations.

Furthermore, the presentation of the scientific ideas and evidence in multivocal, meaning that each youth involved in the project voiced scientific ideas at some point in the movie.

There is also further evidence of social science practices in the movie itself. Interviews with youth, Club staff and other experts indicate the use of ethnographic methods carried out by the youth, and their efforts to allow multiple perspectives shape the broader argument they are making. It matters to them that the student experience (i.e., I do not like cold pizza) and scientific facts and practices (the pizza is served on a non recyclable tray) make up the larger argument they are constructing, indicating their desire to work with complementary but sometimes competing data sets. We believe this also indicates their effort to work with the ambiguity often presented in science, as they sought to make sense across a range of competing data types.

Indeed of the 6 minutes and 11 seconds of the movie, one could easily argue that all but the 10 seconds devoted to the image of the girls performing a fake surgery (in preparation for the section on the lunch dissection) is rich with scientific discourse.

This is true across the four documentaries. Each group presented clear definitions of what a carbon footprint is, offered a framework for how the program under investigation (e.g., canteen or lunch) produced a carbon footprint from initial food production to consumption, provided multiple forms of evidence in support of their points that was both quantitative (e.g., graphs, charts, tables, calculations) and qualitative (e.g., interview data, images, and descriptions). Each group also offered affordable and realistic recommendations to reduce the carbon footprint. Each group also had a clear content story line that made the science fairly easy to understand.

However, the science content story line was engaging through the integration of the youths' personal discourses. For example, in the video described above, the youth interviewed each other informally and expressed their spontaneous opinions about the club's lunch. They wrote raps and prepared music that reflected the content in a playful way, as indicated in the strawberry rap presented on the first page of this chapter. They situated the story in their lives by making connections between the concerns of the neighborhood and the issues emergent in their study.

It can be argued that we engage in hybrid discourses all of the time. We are most interested, however, when the youth combine these discourses in ways that allow them to assert authority – asserting a stance on how and why particular scientific ideas and practices matter. Knowing that youth's products were targeted for an audience that could be broader than just their peers, the youth had to take a position. Therefore any kind of discourse that emphasizes *the youth's position for the issue* was a result of a hybrid discourse that included a major element of authority. For example the position taken in the rap song mentioned at the very beginning of the chapter could be considered an authority discourse which displays the youth' agency or "critical awareness." The rap, though a song that resonated with a personal discourse, also included moments where the participant's agency or position is clearly displayed such as when they say "There is a solution, The solution is to pick strawberries here, They don't have to go far when they are near". Here we sense that they are taking a stance which is that one needs to think of what can be done to decrease the carbon footprint by buying strawberries that are nearby rather than far. Therefore, they are advocating a solution in an assertive manner. They are not only trying to make their argument convincing but going further as to take a stance of what could or should be done. Table 4.1 summarizes the various discourses in the different products.

The different discourses used by the youth were highly regarded by the youth as they allowed for discussion of the issues from various angles. The products utilized the various discourses to state the youth's positions or tell their story. Carbon footprint was the guiding scientific concept and it was one that was used by the four groups at the beginning of their movies. The carbon footprint concept also kept recurring as part of the personal or authority discourse as well. For example the personal discourse was used to move between the different clips that showed the different lunch products. The scientific discourse was revisited in the beginning when defining carbon footprint, it was later included in the middle when they introduced the calculations, and representations, and the authority discourse was mainly prominent in the end where they suggested solutions for the problem.

Table 4.1. Summary of the various discourses for the various groups

	Video 1 *(lunch investigation)*	*Video 2* *(lunch investigation)*	*Video 3* *(canteen investigation)*
Scientific discourse	Defining processing and packaging and showing a bar graph that compares the number of items of lunch processed to those that are not processed	Defining carbon footprint, finding out the chemical, composition of plastic, calculating how much trash is wasted every year in the club	Announcing a scientific definition of carbon footprint, showing the graph for canteen
Personal discourse	Presenting the lunch items and talking about how it is wrapped and processed	Interviews about what club members like in lunch, re-explaining the carbon foot print, information about petroleum and importance of recycling and composting	Showing what's in the canteen, pictures of people and trash, and that "its spicy but not a good thing", in addition to showing how they made chains and purses from candy wrappers
Hybrid discourse based on authority	Giving recommendations to what could be done to decrease carbon foot-print of lunch	Song about local and non-local strawberries, suggestions or recommendations	Recommendations that promoted recycling more, buying local food and planting trees

MORE THAN JUST HYBRID SPACE

More important than the fact that the youth created hybrid spaces is how and why a hybrid authority Discourse seemed to matter to the youth in the nature of their participation. In particular, we believe that the youth sought to create and enact a hybridized discourse that called attention to and elevated the value of their scientific findings among their peers and within their local community. This point is important because of how this kind of hybridity allowed the youth to safely engage in public acts of scientific practice in the middle of a youth-centered, nonacademic social club space. Using hybrid discourses to elevate the value and visibility of science seems to counter some of the research claims that youth engage in hybridity in the effort to maintain personal and social status while also having to engage in academic discourses and practices. Some youth mention that they don't like school science; yet their participation in GET City was very important to them, they keeps showing up and telling us how important and happy they are because they participate in such a program. This suggests that the hybrid discourse we emphasized elevated the importance of science in the lives of youth.

Importance of Hybrid Discourse in the Final Products

Hybrid Discourses shifted the role and value of science by allowing the youth to make a call for action. Such calls for action were "real" and "urgent" and "convincing" by the use of scientific evidence (through representations (graphs), through practices (dissections and surveys), through language choices.)

To illustrate what we mean by real and urgent, we zoom in on the "What's cooking Y'all" video that investigates the canteen. Here, we could see how the whole story line was a hybrid discourse the youth engaged in when trying to present their story in a way that calls for action. The combination of scientific and personal discourses set the stage for their later scene "dissecting the lunch" in which they showed the different packaging items, what they were made of and whether they were recycled or not. All of this happened with chosen music in the background that emphasized the hybrid nature of their product. They found out that most of the items were not recycled, in addition to lack of recycling opportunities at the club. They moved on to stress the importance of eating locally, recycling and using compost bins in active voices (clearly showing what each member wants to say, e.g., B says *Make a compost bin*; P says *use recyclable plastic*). It is an urgent move because without it the carbon footprint is on the rise and this is harmful for the environment. The group worked on this story line for more than a week to plan, gather data and finally produce their movie. While working on this movie they were actively collaborated with one another, researching ideas and composing a rap in order to convince the audience of their case. They ended up with a product that showed how they positioned themselves not only as researchers but also in positions that required their "agency" in order to make assertive claims about the food and the environment in order to induce change. They were in a way the "agents" or "advocates" of this change. The rap that we started the chapter with was included in this movie and it was a signature science artifact (Calabrese Barton, Tan & Rivet, 2008) the girls produced which sustained their agency. While the movie started with a simple presentation of their case, it ends with *real urgent* assertive recommendations that reveals how the authors of this movie took hold of the situation.

The videos also attempted to express a convincing argument by utilizing scientific graphs and representations in addition to social practices of surveys and language choices. Zooming in on the "Green Team" video which probed more closely the club's canteen, we noticed how a hybrid Discourse that is based on scientific Discourse is used to present their case. They started their video by the scientific definition of a carbon footprint after which a picture of the club's canteen was presented. This was followed by a mathematical analysis (pie chart representation) as a result of gathering evidence by surveying their club peers. The pie chart (see Fig. 4.2) presented in the video was constructed by the students as a result of the last question in the survey that the youth used to gather information of how club members use the canteen:

The authors of this video thought that the canteen was "too spicy" and this is not good in terms of the carbon footprint. As a result, they used surveys and interviews to gather information in order to later think of suggestions and recommendations. After presenting the pie chart, they present more evidence in terms of their personal discourses by showing that trucks produce a lot of carbon dioxide and that all items are wrapped in plastic and recycling does not happen. To illustrate this point they utilized another mathematical representation, the bar graph below, that they worked on while investigation how much garbage from canteen is thrown away (Fig. 4.3).

They concluded that out of "22 [types of] sweet snacks, thousands of wrappers in waste." This was an influential slide that is a conclusion by their own language followed by a picture of the contents of a garbage bin containing all the wrappers of those snacks.

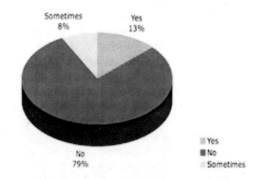

Do You Think Of Your Carbon Footprint When You Buy From The Canteen

Figure 4.2. Evidence of carbon footprint in the canteen program.

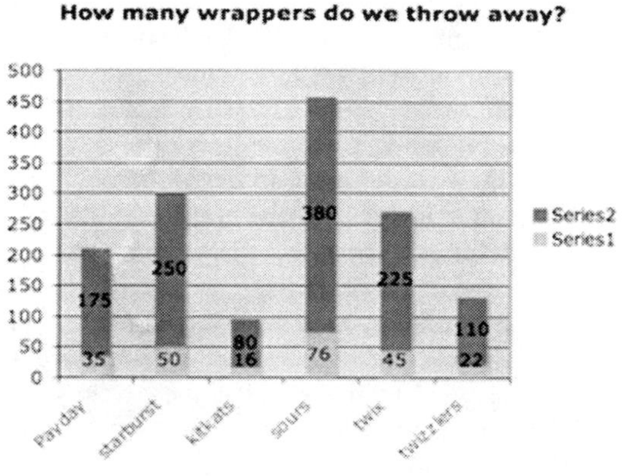

How many wrappers do we throw away?

Figure 4.3. Garbage produced by the canteen daily.

Following that, they switch to a personal discourse where they want to induce change by showing what can be done in order to save all of this trash. They first start by presenting a solution by showing a slide which says: "Candy wrappers are not recyclable you can reuse them." This is followed by showing the steps by which one can reuse them to make purses. They mentioned reducing carbon foot print as part of their personal discourse:

C: If everyone made a purse out of candy wrappers what would that do to carbon footprint?

M: It would reduce pollution and carbon dioxide on the air.

The above dialogue shows that they were constructing an argument using their personal discourse, their idea about making the purse from wrappers and what they knew about the negative effect of a large carbon footprint in order to convince their audience of its importance.

Thinking of the purses as a way to solve this problem seemed important to their identity as teenage girls who are often interested in different kinds of purses and accessories, and believe they can use them and be proud of them. They showed pictures of beautiful purses made of candy wrappers which looked very appealing especially for teenage girls. Another example is when the "Green Team" group thinks of another way and mentions:

Try to find out what your carbon foot print is so you can reduce it
Recycle more
Try to buy local items so the trucks don't cause too much pollution
Plant trees so they will absorb carbon dioxide

These suggestions indicate that the "Green Team" is thinking about natural resources and what's around them as a solution to waste. For example, one of their suggestions is to "Expand the garden at the club, growing more vegetables and using the compost." Such examples of various creative solutions blend what they would like to do and what they are learning about. They are using the science they have engaged in to make an explicit statement about their position concerning the carbon footprint of one's food choices. The representations, technical language, conversations, all help in making this statement and the science they use is meaningful and "friendly". It is meaningful because it is related to something very important in their lives: food and specifically the food they all consume in the club; and "friendly" because the science is helping them better understand the environmental impact of their own food choices as well as helping them make their claims believable to other club members when taking a position as experts. The science then is elevated in the community because the information they learning through science really matters when thinking about food choices in their community. Therefore, science empowers them by providing the evidence to the position they want to take and helps by convincing the audience of their position.

HYBRID DISCOURSE AS A PATHWAY TO COMMUNITY SCIENCE EXPERTISE

In addition to using "hybrid discourse" to spread the word to the community around them, this kind of engagement was also conducive for engaging in legitimate peripheral participation of those issues. The program was not a traditional program where the teaching took place as a whole group and then a paper and pencil test administered to assess knowledge gain. Rather it was one where the issues under discussion and investigation originated from the context the youth were in: the relation of the club's lunch and canteen to the environment. This allowed the youth to be relaxed in proposing their ideas and what they would like to do. Their usage of a "hybrid" Discourse without strictly adhering to any one particular Discourse was an example of how they moved towards legitimate participation. For example, P who is one of "What's cooking Y'all" team members said:

> ... this summer we're learning about like foods, and how they're trans-they're picked and what they're putting them in, and how they're being transported to Michigan to where we are and how many miles and carbon dioxide that they go and use and like how it's harming the uh ozone layer and helping the greenhouses, greenhouse gasses and um, yea, like, that we should get local foods because they don't like, it's, they're local first of all, second of all they don't release a lot of carbon, carbon dioxide and they help the earth, er, it doesn't help it but it stays like the, helps the earth stay the same and doesn't harm it."

In the above interview it shows how this participant could construct an argument about the local food in relation to the environment. She blends the different discourses to make her point, she is actively thinking about the issue. She is the one who thinks that making a compost bin is a good idea and advocates that. She's carrying the ideas further and she mentions:
"Just like they plan for parties, they don't throw a party one hour after they say "I'm gonna throw a party" they, they need to plan about global warming because

the better they conserve our earth the more parties they can get." This participant has been influenced by what they have done over those two weeks that has allowed her to position herself in a situation where she could transfer this discourse to a different situation like organizing a party.

We think that such hybridity supports how youth move in learning from a marginalized position (dispersed and disparate ideas), to a more central position (knowing how to use ideas in other contexts). In addition to that, this participant constantly showed interest in various global issues, like the environment and animal extinction and she mentioned several times during the interview how she watches various TV programs like NOVA science and how those program talk about global warming. Therefore she positions herself as someone who is aware of environmental issues and feels the importance of participating in GET City when she says: "I'll just say it like this: we do more important things, and we get more into it; doesn't mean that we're more important. It means that we do more stuff." This is yet another statement that supports that by using her hybrid discourse (one that she bring with her and one that is engaged in), she was becoming more agentic in her participation.

However, that kind of positioning is not without its complexities, tensions and contradictions which were also detected when talking about those issues. For example the same participant mentioned above was also struggling between "wanting to do the right thing for the environment" and personal needs and desire. This was manifested in several situations during the interview. She said:

> That really got me interested about global warming and everything and I was kinda actually upset that we had to eat local foods because they didn't taste that good. I was, I was wondering whether they could find a way to transport them here without using carbon dioxide, because I still like non-local foods because they taste much better.

The above excerpt shows that although the participant wanted to do the right thing for the environment, that right thing was most probably at odds with her own desires and she felt the tension. She mentions this several times during the interview and she adds on at one point: "I'll try and put up with local foods, although the local tomatoes are fantastic, um, but sometimes I just wish it were different." This tension illustrates the struggle between her personal preference and what she's adamant of, which is doing what's good for the environment; however she is willing to "put up" with local food which shows the influence of the ideas on her. Such remarks were quite frequent though among other youth. Another participant mentioned in the interview:

> I was upset because non-local foods tasted much better. I don't know whether it's because they stayed longer or maybe some of the air that, that, or the compost or something in California is, or Ohio or Wisconsin is better than the one in Michigan. It's just that all the fruits and- well the chocolate didn't make a difference, but for the fruits and vegetables, it made a difference.

She continued to say that taste matters to her and if she thought that non-local food tasted better, then eating local food "I would not get that good taste" as she puts it. Such remarks are ones that we occasionally heard: youth liked certain kinds of foods and choices even though such choices were not so environmentally friendly. When we were discussing the milk jugs, one participant mentioned that his father had tried to buy the newly produced milk jugs which have a lower carbon footprint but found such jugs impractical when it comes to pouring and reverting to old jugs. This kind of tension and confusion is a genuine quandary for most of the environmental issues and especially in the club's complex social environment where peer pressure and long time habits are major factors in the youth's lives. It is the kind of tension that most people face, and for this student to be expressing such views indicates the authenticity of her experiences with the topic. As much as our youth have engaged in pro-environmentally friendly activities, they are also human beings with their own preferences. In this matter, the program's objective was not to "convert" individuals but to allow for the complexity of the issue to unravel, as shown by the above examples. Referring to Lave and Wenger's legitimate peripheral participation we can say that the participant was able to start as a legitimate peripheral participant but move on to center stage to "live" the experience with the knowledge, creativity, and complexity that she was engaged with.

WHY WOULD EXPERIENCING A HYBRID DISCOURSE REALLY MATTER?

We have argued that youth in GET City program have had opportunities to blend discourses and create a "hybrid space" where they express their own ideas as well as explore other ideas in order to participate in a discourse about the carbon footprint of one's food choices, which is relevant to their lives. We think that such participation has started out marginally, but with time has moved on to a center position where youth were the main players in deciding what is important. The expression of their views took place by blending personal, scientific and authoritative discourse. During those five weeks, we think that the youth have moved with issues to a "central" position as a result of participating in a program that capitalized on the youth' ideas, on their concrete live experiences, and on the different technological, educational and human resources they were exposed to. Consequently, the youth exercised "agency" when they utilized "hybrid discourse" to present their case. This experience, however, was not without tension when they thought really hard about transferring those ideas to their everyday habits which is a "legitimate" product of such "legitimate peripheral participation" as Lave and Wenger (1991) would argue and as Gutierrez (2008) would claim: "By attending to the microgenetic processes of everyday learning across a range of contexts, with one eye focused on the collective and the other on individual sense making activity, we can note new forms of activity, stimulated by unresolved tensions or dilemmas, that can lead to rich cycles of learning." However this tension could be seen as a positive tension where new positioning afforded by hybridity allows and supports youth to delve more deeply into socio-environmental issues such as making decisions about what to eat when one is mindful of one's carbon footprint. One could see that as a positive tension that youth are struggling with: it allows them to appreciate the many factors that affect peoples' food decisions. We see this as a positive learning outcome where the participant is identifying with different arguments relevant to this issue, which positions him or her in a more informed position to be an agent about this issue.

NOTES

[1] We use Discourse with a capital D to reference communication patterns that reflect ways of being and knowing, that is related to one's identity, as opposed to discourse with a small d that references conversation or talk that one uses without its strong connection to identity (Gee, 1999).

BHASKAR UPADHYAY AND NANCY ALBRECHT

5. DELIBERATIVE DEMOCRACY IN AN URBAN ELEMENTARY SCIENCE CLASSROOM

Over a one-week period a fourth-grade class is investigating the question: What things does a bean seed need to germinate? The students created a list of items such as water, dirt, light, and, air that the bean seed will need to germinate. Each student placed their bean seeds in a plastic cup covered by wet cotton balls and observed the seeds grow for a week. The following week students shared their observations and discussed the outcomes. Here we will present a short discussion between three students related to bean seed germination:

Dashaun: My seed has a little thing coming out of seed [root] and seed has white thing [seed coat] tear. My seed doesn't smell like Arian's because it is growing.

Ayana: *I want to add* what Dashaun said. [Pause] My seed has little thing growing and it's not smelling. Growing seed doesn't smell. We also soak seed in water to germinate quickly.

Kiona: *I don't agree* with Dashaun and Ayana because my seed is growing and the growing part is brown. My seed is growing and it is brown color and don't smell. Dashaun and Ayana seed grow but different color. I want to ask Ayana: We didn't soak seeds to germinate?

Ayana: *I disagree* with Kiona because if seed doesn't grow it smell like Maria's. Her seed has no growing part and look sticky and smell. My seed and Dashaun seed are growing and don't smell. At home we soak seed first and put them in dirt because it grow fast.

Dashaun, Ayana, and Kiona were discussing their findings based on what they observed from their respective experiments. Dashaun presented his findings and used evidence from his experiment that if seeds grow they don't smell. He saw that seeds that germinate should not smell. Ayana agreed with Dashaun and added her evidence to support Dashaun's claims. On the other hand Kiona disagreed with Dashaun and Ayana's claims because Kiona saw that the color of the germinating part of the seed was associated with smell. Kiona believes that color of the root system that grows out of the seeds make a difference too. Ayana completely disagreed with Kiona's claim about the connection between the color of the root and the smell because Ayana observed that her friend Maria's seeds smelled bad because it was dead.

In this example fourth-grade students are engaged in science discourse that shows how well they use evidence from their experiments and also knowledge

S.J. Basu et al., (eds.), Democratic Science Teaching: Building the Expertise to Empower Low-Income Minority Youth in Science, 75–87.

from their home experiences. The most intriguing aspect of this discussion is that students respectfully agree and disagree with their friends' points of views. Dashaun and Ayana are presented new or similar evidence from their friends' experiments that supported their claims that correlated seed germination to smell. Both Dashaun and Ayana asserted that if seeds are germinating then they shouldn't smell bad. On the other hand Kiona related germination to the color.

Furthermore, Ayana interjected her own knowledge about how soaking the seeds before planting could help them germinate easily and quicker. Even though in the class they didn't soak the seeds in the water before planting, Ayana felt free to share her knowledge about seed germination that she learned at home. However, Kiona questioned the connection between Ayona's knowledge about soaking seeds to help seeds germinate easily with what they were discussing. Kiona was correct to point out that since they did not soak the seeds before they started their experiments, they should discount Ayona's new idea about soaking the seeds before planting.

Dashaun, Ayana, and Kiona understand that differences among their ideas and the evidence that they use to support their claims are essential parts of doing and learning science in their classroom. Finally, the decision made by the class with the support from the teacher plays an important role in establishing and learning in a democratic classroom.

In the example, Dashaun, Ayana, and Kiona engaged in a discussion based on sound reasoning. The back and forth nature of the discussions between Ayana and Kiona as to what amounts to germination of the bean seeds are essential aspects of deliberative democracy. In elementary schools students need to participate in this kind of open discussion to make science learning more authentic and useful. That means a deliberative democratic classroom environment is essential in better science learning.

DELIBERATIVE DEMOCRACY AND SCHOOL SCIENCE

In an ideal context deliberative democracy is about democratic association where individuals participate in the resolution of common problems through public reasoning within an institution that the participants believe in. In this regard deliberative democracy encompasses five important features as it is practiced (Young 2001; Gutmann & Thompson 2004): 1) deliberation is an on-going process; 2) equal voice and equal participation among individuals; 3) diverse ideals, convictions, and preferences are valued; 4) legitimate institutions promote and support deliberative practices; and 5) all individuals are capable of contributing in the deliberative practices.

Some scholars of deliberative democracy argue that in the context of everyday classroom, deliberative democracy is very difficult to sustain because of myriads of constraints that a classroom teacher has to overcome (Fishkin & Luskin, 2005). For example in an inner city urban elementary school teachers are more worried about completing the State Standards for the required state tests; lack of resources to do science in the classrooms; more focus and time spent on language and math proficiency; science is relegated to one more subject to be taught when there is enough time left from language and mathematics; high turnover rate in students and families; high number of students with ethnic, racial, and linguistic diversity; and high teacher turnover rate. Because of these reasons many students who attend inner city urban schools tend to have low classroom participation. Additionally, some students may consider argumentation socially unacceptable behavior and show low level of engagement in the classroom discussions (Mutz, 2006). For example in Native American and Hmong cultures argumentation is an impolite and undesired social behavior which may discourage students from these and similar groups with similar cultural values to engage in science learning (Aikenhead, 1997; Upadhyay, 2006).

One of the major goals of National Science Education Standards is to promote the understanding of dynamic process of knowledge construction through inquiry teaching learning practices in science at the K-12 level. K-12 science standards put very high emphasis on science teaching and learning where students build their skills to understand and use evidenced based reasoning skills; connect science to everyday experiences and knowledge; and value diverse ideas and knowledge as assets to learning science (NRC, 1996; Warren, Ogonowski & Pothier, 2005). Therefore, inquiry teaching and learning demands that students engage in the process of reason giving, whereby each student gets to participate actively and to add a distinct perspective. The inquiry-learning environment requires students to deliberate their science understanding continuously based on the evidence they gather from their activities and from their own lived experience. An environment of dynamic discussion in the science classroom also helps to create opportunities for students and teachers to continue discussions that strengthen and enhance student learning in science. Furthermore, in a deliberative democratic environment, some students may not agree with the final decision, but they are more likely to accept the decisions because their arguments were heard and were given an appropriate place in the collective decision-making process.

An important component of deliberative democracy is access to knowledge and the use of that knowledge in learning. Deliberative democracy can be an asset in a science classroom because it encourages the use of content knowledge both from home and standard science classrooms that is accessible to the students involved. Deliberative democracy depends on knowledgeable citizens, and so all content related to an issue must be presented so that all citizens can understand it. Similarly, the goal of science education is to make science knowledge accessible to all students and to improve understanding of science content for all students. Students who are knowledgeable in science can participate in civic discourse related, for example, to such issues as community and environment, pollution, global warming, and health, and can participate both inside and outside the classroom. Knowing and understanding science content allows students to participate in science discussions and to openly defend and refine their positions, based on their peers' and teacher's counter-reasons and arguments. In a deliberative democratic classroom students are continuously provided a space to present their arguments in order to come to a universal decision that fits their learning goals.

For this study, we investigated two important aspects of deliberative democracy as it was implemented in an elementary science classroom. First, we looked at how elementary students engaged in the deliberative process in a science classroom. Second, we documented the ways that deliberative democracy is empowering to students from disadvantaged communities.

LEARNING ABOUT STUDENTS AND SCHOOL CONTEXTS

We worked with elementary students in a very poor part of Minneapolis since 2007. Most of the residents in North Minneapolis are African American or are immigrants from North Africa, Asia, and South and Central America. We engaged with teachers and students of Hope Elementary on a gardening project intended to help students learn science and science skills. The project was also intended to make an empty lot behind the school aesthetically attractive. The school and parents were concerned that youth were using the space to hang out during school hours instead of attending school, and that youth from other neighborhoods were using the space for drug activities. During this time, we observed 25 lessons, recorded 18 group interactions as the students engaged in science investigations, and conducted eight focus group interviews with each group, which lasted about one hour each time we met. For this chapter, we focused on a group of students who modeled deliberative democracy better than other groups. Ms. J, their teacher, made clear to students that the science classroom is a place for learning science through investigation in an open and dialogic manner.

Our analysis is based on existing literature on democracy in K-12 classroom settings. First, we looked for statements and actions from the students that related to the concepts of democracy and science, such as arguments, multiple knowledge roots such as home, school, media, etc., and the social implications of science. These statements and actions were put into themes, such as evidenced-based arguments and cultural knowledge and norms.

DELIBERATING FOR A GARDEN

Fourth-grade students in Ms. J's class at Hope Elementary[1] are taught science for thirty minutes daily. The thirty-minute science lesson takes place at the end of the school day. Ms. J starts the science lesson promptly, and prepares science lessons days ahead, in order to make the best use of her time with the students. Most of her students are from poor African-American families, and some are from Hmong immigrant families. Her students are clearly excited about learning science and about doing science investigations.

In early March of 2007, Ms. J told her students that they would get to grow different kinds of plants and vegetables in science class. Since the summer in the Midwest is short, they would work inside to get ready to plant what they wanted outside in mid-May, if the weather was warm enough by then. Ms. J had students work in groups of five to come up with detailed plans for their garden. She also mentioned that they would get to use grow lights in the class to investigate every-thing about growing, and so that they could start their gardens as soon as the weather got warm for the plants. On a white chart, Ms. J listed the questions that students needed to answer in the next five weeks: 1) What kind of soil do you need for plants to grow?; 2) What kinds of plants (vegetables, herbs, flowers, etc.) do you want to grow and why?; 3) How do you know which plants will grow well in Minnesota?; and 4) What kind of environment do the plants need to grow well? Ms. J told them, "You have to decide all this."

The group of students that we followed had three girls and two boys. Jimmy and Annie come from Hmong families and Quintin, Sarah, and Kim come from African-American families. After Ms. J's instructions, the group began the task of planning their garden.

The discussions reveals disagreement on how a raised bed should look and how it should be divided into sections. Two students disagree on when they should divide their plots and how they should divide to grow different plants. Quintin interjects that doing science demands that they follow steps to complete their tasks. However, Sarah disagrees that science has to be done in defined steps, and she further supports her argument by stating, "growing and designing plots are not related." Sarah's understanding of scientific processes indicates that she has a very good understanding of how science is done – that science does not have *the method*. Seeing the disagreement between Quintin and Sarah, Annie tries to act like a mediator by suggesting that they could come back and still divide the plots as suggested by Sarah.

Quintin believes that drainage and time are two important issues that need resolving if they are to agree to Annie's suggestion of making a raised bed. Quintin insists that "drainage is still the issue." Additionally, Quintin makes it clear to the group that the drainage is an important issue to be resolved because they learned in the science class earlier that "water [clogged] soil will kill the plants." Water-clogged soil does not allow air to circulate in the soil, depriving vital oxygen for the roots to survive and provide water and nutrients for a plant. Therefore, he is not happy with the raised bed. Agreeing with Quintin's concerns, Annie suggests that they test different soil samples, including the one from the garden outside to see if the garden soil has good drainage. Students like Annie are able to add their knowledge from home about the raised beds to the knowledge gained in science class. Furthermore, Annie also taps into parental expertise to help design the best-raised bed: "My father make [made] big holes in the wood and put in the garden. I think this [holes] will work [drain water]. I can ask my father to help us to cut wood and make holes."

Students are deliberating to decide how they should design their raised bed so that the plants that they will grow can thrive. The focus of deliberative activity is to arrive at a solution that is acceptable to the group. The goal is to design a garden that will allow the students to understand what factors influence how plants grow and how to decide which plants to grow. Ms. J designed the class, and empowered students to have discussions that will led to appropriate decisions about gardening and planting, based on their prior science knowledge and also the data that they collect during the process. It is also clear from the student discussions that they have studied materials related to plants, and factors that influence plant growth, such as the necessary amount of water and air flow around the roots of plants.

Another aspect of a deliberative discussion is a reflection on one's prior know-ledge gained at school or at home. Hmong students reveal how their knowledge about raised beds can contribute to an improved raised bed at school. Annie, a Hmong student, also offers to bring the human resources and skills of her parents to help make a proper raised bed.

LISTENING TO AND VALUING OF OTHERS' IDEAS IN A SCIENCE CLASSROOM

When four students in Ms. J's class enrolled at Hope Elementary in January, stories were added to the classroom board. Ms. J asked students to read the story of each group member before the groups could start working on the new science topics on plant, soil, factors influencing plant growth, weather, and gardening. Out of five students in the group that I (Bhaskar) was observing on this day, Jimmy and Kim were new transfer students.

Last week (March 18, 2008) Quintin, Sarah, Jimmy, Kim, and Annie decided which vegetables they wanted to grow in their garden. They all agreed on Quintin and Sarah's idea that they should grow pumpkin because it would be ready for Halloween and everyone in the group could take one home or carve the pumpkin in their art class: "…Then we can like make [carve] some cool animals or African art or like Annie and Jimmy's arts [Hmong arts]." During this class discussion students in the group shared diverse ideas about why growing pumpkin is a good choice. The students' comments not only demonstrate the learning process for science content related to environment, pollution, and health but also show that what students do and learn in science is connected to their lives. Doing science is more personal than just completing a science task efficiently and as expected by the teacher, a more traditional science classroom requirement. Sarah and Quintin are not only concerned about the science of gardening, but also what that learning means to their personal needs. They both talk about how their work in learning science through gardening also accomplishes an economic benefit that they had not thought about earlier. Quintin in particular elaborates on why growing pumpkin is such an important act beyond learning science. He shows concern that his father lost a job and that the family is having a hard time making ends meet. Becoming a regular visitor to the community food shelters has taken a toll on him, leading him to worry about how his parents will provide for him his siblings. The hardships he faces are explicitly expressed, and his stress persists at school despite the more secure environment (e.g., a school lunch). Quintin is speaking not just for himself but also for his friends in the class who may have a similar situation at home but have not spoken about it yet, or just do not feel safe to share their situation with others. Quintin talks about sharing the produce with his class peers and with their floor janitor and Ms. J: "Share pumpkin with others in the class and give one to Ms. J and Mr. Donald." In this case, doing science becomes an integral part of life-worlds that students are going through or have been through. For Quintin, science has a particular relevance to his current situation and he sees science as a subject that is worth participating in and learning. Quintin's comments and his drive to convince the members of his group to grow pumpkin is very deliberate and well reasoned. He not only gives economic reasons but also recalls Ms. J's comments about how much care each vegetable needs to bear fruit. He adds a logical point that pumpkin might be the best option because it needs less care compared to other vegetables that they could grow, which is important in the summer when they are out of school and have less access to their garden. This enhances the science content knowledge the class is attaining, regarding what conditions plants need in order to grow (such as sunlight, water, and minerals) and how much they need these essential ingredients to grow well.

Jimmy and Annie view learning to garden an admirable and valuable skills set, since it connect to their Hmong culture and values and learning these science concepts could enhance skills that they can put to practical use in their family or community. They do not seem to be concerned with what vegetables the group decides to grow, but are very interested in learning about gardening. For them, knowledge about gardening is as important as learning science concepts related to plants, land ecosystems, and soil, as they express in their discussion. This kind of interest is essential to learning science and later being successful in science, if they choose to go into the field.

In the process of deliberating their choice for pumpkin farming, students were able to draw upon and relate to doing and learning science that was relevant to social, personal, cultural, and economic issues. Sarah, Quintin, Jimmy, Annie, and Kim demonstrated the characteristics of a deliberative democratic science classroom that produces enlightened knowledge rather than just required knowledge. Another important aspect of this discussion is the space that was given to each member of the group to share his/her own reasons for agreeing to grow pumpkin. Sarah and Quintin focused their comments on economic advantage and carving; and Jimmy and Annie focused on learning gardening skills that made their parents happy. These diverse views were talked about, listened to, appreciated, and valued by students who were in some ways strangers to each other because they still did not know much about each other. In this discussion, students' shared broad reasons and ideas related to the issue of what plants to grow. These broad ideas stemmed from the students' diverse social perspectives and social positions, thus aiding to develop social knowledge that otherwise would not have been conveyed to other group members. From a broader perspective, students were not only helping each other master the traditional academic science curriculum, but were also engaged in being resources for each other's learning. Students in Ms. J's class also experienced a public decision-making process in which individuals from diverse and lesser known groups collaborated to understand and find a solution to shared problems – in this case doing and learning science concepts related to plant science, soil science, pollution, and variables through gardening.

SCIENCE INQUIRY AND DEMOCRATIC SOCIAL COOPERATION

Science inquiry promotes alternative explanations and interpretations related to science concepts, thus generating a broader science understanding. In the inquiry process, broader interpretations and explanations play an essential role in science learning. These diverse sets of interpretations and explanations are possible only when there is social cooperation among the individuals in a classroom.

Ms. J had taught students that animal protein from chickens, cows, and pigs are costly to the environment, and had described the length of time farmers take to raise animals for meat or milk. Ms. J introduced the food pyramid concept, and explained that their school lunch program is "based on [food pyramid]." Ms. J wanted all the groups to grow beans, but she left each group to decide the type of bean to grow. She also wanted the groups to investigate the rate of growth for each type of bean (pinto, black, kidney, fava, string, etc.), the water-retention capacity of different types of soil, and how fast each kind of bean germinated.

After a decision to grow string beans, Quintin, Sarah, Jimmy, Kim, and Annie deliberated which variety of string beans would give the greatest yield and have the fastest growth rate, and conducted a thorough and careful consideration of the issues. For three weeks after deciding the kind of vegetables to grow, they tested string bean seeds from different companies to see which were best suited to their garden. The group had earlier agreed that they would not use the names of the brands because they could "find things [information] about beans and companies that packed them and that may give clues which beans will grow fast and which slow. If we know answer before experimenting we can just looking [for] answers" [Kim, March, 2008]. Kim raised a point about experimenting in science and looking for an answer. She was sharing an important aspect of science that their findings can be biased because of what they already know about plant growth, seeds, and germination. She was also making her group members aware that since they knew a lot about plant growth through their online research and from science reference books, they would be able to record important observations related to seed germination and growth. However, she cautioned that they would have to be careful not to document anything that they did not see, because they may be tempted to fit the data to what they hoped to find. For Kim, science appeared to be about evidence-based findings, and the fact that she was able to make that point in the group is an important demonstration of a democratic classroom. Similar sentiments were expressed when Jimmy and Annie added to Kim's comment that if they knew which companies produced "bad seeds," they might not do their experiment properly like the "real scientists," and their garden project decisions would be based on evidence that was not from the experiment. In this deliberation, Kim, Jimmy and Annie established a framework for conducting their science experiment and for how evidence from the experiment should guide their decisions.

Once the results on bean plant germination and growth were collected, they deliberated on the evidence to reach the final decision on which string bean variety to grow in their raised bed. The group is deliberating in order to agree to which beans grow the fastest, and which seeds produce the most beans when planted in their raised bed. Jimmy starts the deliberation by presenting the evidence on how many string beans grew. Since all five string bean seeds from different brands (p1 & p3) germinated and grew, Jimmy argues that these seeds are better than seeds from other two brands p2 and p4. However, Sarah presents a counter-argument, disagreeing with

Jimmy asserting that, since they are looking for the fastest growing string beans, p2 should be the choice because one of the string bean seeds grew to be 7 centimeters, the tallest of all the string beans tested. Kim argues that most of the seeds grew to a height of about 5 centimeters, but one bean seed that grew to be 7 centimeters. Kim feels that they can't base their decision on just one 7-centimeter string-bean plant, but should look at the average growth of each brand of bean, and decide which grew the fastest. Annie argues that on average, the height of the bean plants from the p3 brand were similar to that of other brands that they had tested. Annie adds her home experience to support her claim that bean seeds from the p3 brand are better, because her grandmother always uses the p3 brand of seeds because these string beans handle the change in weather conditions better. Finally, Kim argues that "you have to take all the things like all germinating, all growing together and live in bad weather" into account to make the decision because the beans will have to grow well outside in the elements, and not in a controlled environment as was the case with their experiment. The group agrees to string bean seeds from the p3 brand based on the evidence from their experiment and on anecdotal evidence from Annie's home, which was convincing.

In this case, Kim utilizes Annie's knowledge of string beans to make the case for the brand of string beans the group should choose. The group values and pays attention to the knowledge from another culture, in this case Hmong, as an important source of evidence to make the decision. The group not only participates in authentic science but also deliberates based on authentic data.

DISCUSSION

As Jimmy, Sarah, Quintin, Kim, and Annie investigated many aspects of gardening and of their future garden, they deliberated systematically and thoroughly when it came to deciding what they wanted in their garden. We described above some successful aspects of deliberative democracy enacted in an elementary science classroom. There are three important components of deliberative democracy in an elementary science classroom setting that emerge from this research: (1) evidence-based argument or reason-giving; (2) equity in participation and decision making; and (3) respect and value for others' cultural knowledge. We discuss each component.

Evidence-based Argument: Home and School Knowledge

One of the key goals of science education at the elementary level is to ensure that students understand the importance of evidence in science. Students also need to understand that new science knowledge is created based on new evidence. Most elementary students engage in confirmatory science, where the goal is to understand well-established, existing science concepts through evidence gathered in the class-room. Elementary students have to learn not only how to gather evidence, but how to use that evidence to support their arguments during classroom deliberations. Thus, scientific argument is not about winning or losing, but instead involves sharing, processing, and building a deeper understanding of science content. For example, Sarah, Annie, Jimmy, and Kim deliberate on which brand of string beans they should plant in their raised-bed garden. They understand that the summer in Minnesota is short, and so they needed to choose variety of string bean that grew fastest in order to harvest the crop easily. As they deliberated different brands of string beans, they drew on evidence they had gathered from their experiment. They had gathered data not only on the height of each brand of string bean, but also on the time to germinate, the number of seeds that died without germinating, the place of each bean in the clay pot, the temperature of soil throughout the experiment, the number of leaves on each string bean plant, and they had recorded qualitative descriptions of each plant, such as how the plant looked (e.g., healthy, weak, or strong). Students in the group interpreted the same data differently. Jimmy's argument for the p2 brand of string beans was based on a single string bean seed that grew to be the tallest. He reasoned that if one bean shows that kind of growth, all the bean seeds from that brand should have the same quality. His evidence was based on one piece of data, thus choosing selectively what counted as evidence to support his argument. Annie momentarily concurred with Jimmy, but quickly changed her mind because she found Jimmy's evidence less plausible. She also used her grandmother's experience and years of knowledge about different varieties of string beans and how well they grow in adverse environments. Similarly, Kim's argument for string beans from the p3 brand was founded on both the evidence from their investigation and the knowledge from Annie's grandmother. Thus, the deliberation on the choice of string beans was mostly anchored on evidence from class investigation and knowledge from the experience of Annie's grandmother. We saw similar evidenced-based reasoning continue during later science investigations and discussions in the class.

On the other hand, the nature of argument in social settings such as family, friend, and politics generally tends to gravitate towards defending one's ideological ideas or beliefs without much evidence. Thus, arguments in social contexts tend to focus more on winning or losing (Michaels, O'Connor & Resnick, 2008). This kind of dichotomy in argument does not help students learn science or the core value of evidence in scientific enterprises. Ms. J is very specific about distinguishing what *argument* means in science, and how important it is to have evidence to support or dispute an argument. In Ms. J's class, we consistently heard her tell the students that they needed to have some kind of data or evidence, either from their own investigation or from their textbook and reference books, that she would not let them just speak. She also regularly reminds them that evidence is their friend in science and that it is through evidence that they will understand science content and concepts. We have also seen students regularly ask their peers to show where they "got the results [data/evidence]." Ms. J's deliberative democratic science classroom clearly helps to promote an attitude in students that highly values evidence-based argument.

Equity in Participation and Decision-Making

In inquiry-based science teaching and learning, students are engaged in scientific investigations to understand science concepts and process skills. This requires students to participate in discussions, deliberations, and decision-making processes so that they can successfully investigate science ideas and questions. Teachers have traditionally relied on a classroom participation format known as IRE, or Initiation (I) of a question or task by a teacher, Response (R) by student/s, and Evaluation (E) of the response/s by the teacher (Cazden, 1988), because this format allows teachers to control the direction of the classroom discussion and to evaluate students' learning at the same time. This kind of participation format limits students' participation, however, beyond giving responses and getting the correct answer to the questions posed. When students are deliberating on a science investigation or topic, they are seeking opportunities to present their arguments and listen to the counter arguments supported by evidence. Thus, there has to be a dynamic process of participation in a deliberative democratic classroom.

Students come from different cultural and social values, which affect their inter-actions with peers, their actions in group settings, and their responses to teacher comments and questions (Lee, 2002; Lipka, 1998). As with culture in general, where there are acceptable norms for communication, science has its own norms for participating through talk and text (Aikenhead & Jegede, 1999). This in turn will encourage all students to actively share their ideas and help in the collective decision-making process.

Equity in participation in a democratic classroom is also evident from the fact that students in this class interrupted each other in the middle of an argument to present their cases, and there was no predetermined sequence for speaking. Additionally students participated in very high frequency (based on the video and observation data used for this chapter), for example, Quintin talked on eight occasions; Sarah talked on thirteen occasions; Annie talked on nine occasions; Jimmy talked on eight occasions; and Kim talked on nine occasions. Similar frequency of participation was observed among these five individuals during the course of their investigations and engagement in learning science through gardening. However, frequency of participation does not indicate a sustained high-quality deliberation. One of the difficult issues in the practice of deliberative democracy in classroom settings is assessing the quality of argumentation (Chambers 2003).

Gender equity in participation and in the decision-making process is evident too. The girls in the group actively participated in the decision-making process and presented compelling arguments for and against various positions. Kim seemed to show particularly active participation among the girls, basing her arguments on evidence; as a result, she appeared to have a greater influence on the decision-making process. There seemed to be equal respect for girls' as for boys' ideas. Dominance among the students did not seem to be based on gender. In many science class-rooms, students from minority groups and low socio-economic status (SES) families struggle to have an equitable opportunity to participate in classroom discussions. Many of these students are shut out because their input is considered inferior by peers and teachers from the majority group. Students from minority and low SES groups also feel constrained due to language and cultural differences from equitable participation in the decision-making process.

Valuing and Respecting the Knowledge of Others

Classrooms are not neutral. Students' relationship to their culture and knowledge gained from experience are not suspended to learn new knowledge at school.

Classrooms include students from diverse social, linguistic, and cultural backgrounds, making them a dynamic and challenging learning environment. Teaching in a diverse school setting is even more complex in science classrooms because, for many students, scientific language is new and difficult to decipher. One way to help students engage in science is to allow them to bring their knowledge from their own experience into the classroom. The combination of science and home knowledge provides a better basis for the understanding of science content and concepts.

Deliberative democracy can only be successful when participants value and respect each others' cultural knowledge. Although the interruptions among students looked disorganized on the surface, upon closer inspection it becomes clear that the arguments engaged in by Quintin, Sarah, and Kim were highly productive and related to their task. This suggests that a deliberative democratic classroom environment allowed Quintin, Sarah, and Kim to learn in an environment that was familiar to them. For Jimmy and Annie, the fact that their cultural norms of interactions were valued by other group members allowed them to experience a sense of belonging and to learn science in a way that felt familiar.

The group deliberated on why they should grow pumpkin and how that was connected to their personal needs and immediate lives. This is critical, since a process that is not connected to personal experience or does not hold the promise of future personal benefits, discourages learning. Many scholars have empirically shown that a personal connection to science learning has a strong correlation to better understanding, and to the long-term retention of science knowledge (Calabrese Barton, 1998; Bouillion & Gomez, 2001; Upadhyay, 2006). Quintin believed that growing pumpkin would help his parents financially so that they wouldn't have to buy a pumpkin for Halloween. Later, as the group engaged in other investigations and learned different science concepts connected to gardening, plants, and the environment, Quintin was excited to learn the concepts, as he noted in his journal: "Now I see how science can help me and other friends. Like growing pumpkin helps us learn about soil, plant life cycle, and help us by saving money."

In this case, students talked about other salient discourses such as economy when learning science. Students connected growing pumpkin to ethnic arts, economy, and the implications to the environment and their communities. These personal examples relate science to social and political situations that influence communities like those of Kim and Annie. If students learn how to deliberate and present scientific evidence to support their positions in a classroom setting, it will help them to participate in larger social and political discourse. Thus, a deliberative democratic science classroom environment empowers students to be active participants outside the classroom.

Just as Dashaun, Ayona, and Kiona present a dynamic and personally connected science learning experiences in a democratic science classroom Quintin, Sarah, Jimmy, Kim, and Annie represent a complex nature of deliberative democracy where elementary students in an urban science class. At the elementary school level, the students may not be as sophisticated as in later grades, and might not sustain complex and high-quality arguments and counter-arguments. However, this study shows that elementary students in science classes are capable of interacting and benefitting from a deliberative democratic process. Of particular note from the study is that elementary students are capable of presenting evidence-based arguments and of convincing their peers or strangers in the classroom setting. Another important aspect of enacting a deliberative democratic process in a science classroom is that it allows students to utilize knowledge from their lived experience and builds confidence to participate more actively. Students feel empowered as they are able to present their arguments without much constraint, and to have a sense of equity in learning science. Thus, deliberative democracy, though it has many constraints that are difficult to measure effectively in a science classroom setting, helps to empower students to engage in and learn science.

NOTES

[1] All names are pseudonyms to protect the identities of the participants and the school.

GALE SEILER

6. TEACHING FOR DEMOCRATIC RECONSTRUCTION

A Science Classroom in Rural South Africa

The 1994 election marked the end of apartheid in South Africa. Since then, the government and the people of South Africa have been striving to bring to life a vision of democracy. From the start, the role of education in this democratic project has been prominent. The establishment of participatory democracy on local and national levels has been seen as crucial to democratic development, and education has been re-envisioned with the intention both to promote and mirror democratic principles. Yet education remains one area that suffers tremendously under the historical legacy of apartheid and faces difficult odds, particularly in rural areas.

Jhumki Basu spent time in South Africa during July and August of 2003, working as part of a mobile physics outreach program called Physics Emasondosondo, which visited township and rural schools in Gauteng province. This was a traveling program intended both to excite learners[1] about physics and also provide some opportunities for hands-on experimental work. It had been designed through the collaboration of South African teachers and university and ministry personnel.

The Emasondosondo team comprised roughly equal numbers of American and South African participants (college students, high school educators, and one or two scientists) and ran for about six weeks. The traveling program visited one school per day and spent the day working with high school students and their teachers. Jhumki was particularly active in the working with the teachers. She worked to develop teacher support materials and to provide guidance on the use of the basic science equipment that was left at each school after a visit.

As the program developed and grew, the South African investment became greater so the program would become fully locally sustained. It continues to operate success-fully, running essentially year-round, and has also served as a model for other traveling science initiatives in South Africa.

In 2003, when she worked on Physics Emasondosondo, Jhumki had only recently been treated for her initial breast cancer. She was taking medication throughout the time in South Africa, but was characteristically determined to work extremely hard throughout. As Jeremy Dodd of Columbia University, who also worked on the project explained, "[w]e did not talk too much at that time about the larger issues surrounding science education in developing countries and with underserved populations, how-ever in retrospect I think that Jhumki's time working in disadvantaged South African high schools helped shape her subsequent path" (Dodd, personal communication).

S.J. Basu et al., (eds.), Democratic Science Teaching: Building the Expertise to Empower Low-Income Minority Youth in Science, 89–101.

Like Jhumki's work in South Africa, my work in that country has been brief, spanning eight weeks in July and August of both 2008 and 2009. However, unlike Jhumki, I went to South Africa late in my career rather than early. I had been a high school science teacher in the United States for 17 years and a university professor for six years, and my interest in social justice in science education was on-going. Despite many years of experience in education, I still questioned what I could offer to the South African educators and learners that I encountered in this context of which I understood so little. I questioned the universality of phrases such as social justice in science education and transformative and democratic science education.

Jhumki's work explored how definitions of democratic science pedagogy in the literature contrasted with enactment of it in classrooms. It was her belief that teaching and learning are meaningful, authentic and just when they are more than a set of top-down prescriptions and instead reflect the beliefs, ideas and creativity of the teachers and students involved in practice. This chapter explores what democratic science education might mean in a historico-political context outside the United States, such as post-apartheid South Africa, and considers the extent to which definitions of democratic education are universal.

The end of apartheid in 1994 signaled profound changes to the education system in South Africa, including the way science teaching would be done in schools serving African students. But occurrences since then raise questions of power and the emergence of exclusive forms of science. In South African communities where the memory of resistance to oppression and violence is so fresh and where democratic practice is so new, what form can democratic schooling and science education take?

POST-APARTHEID EDUCATION[2]

Before 1994, the education system in South Africa with its Christian national education and Bantustan education policies effectively deprived the African populations of obtaining a quality education, especially in the areas of mathematics and science where few African students acquired qualifications. For many years, African students were significantly disadvantaged compared to Whites based on pupil-teacher ratios, per pupil expenditures, and percentage of qualified teachers, and this was reflected in huge disparities in performance, for example, in Standard 10 (Grade 12) examination pass rates (Hofmeyer and Buckland, 1992). Certainly, great change was needed in education in South Africa, and the new democratic govern-ment responded with three waves of radical reform in just a few years. Pre-1994, drastically different curricula were taught in White schools and African schools. The African students in rural areas were seen only as laborers and received a very narrow and limited curriculum intended to keep them out of white-collar jobs. In 1996 South Africa passed the South African Schools Act to ensure that all learners would have access to education without discrimination. A new national curriculum, called Curriculum 2005, was introduced in 1997 with the goal of providing a common curriculum for all schools, thus removing the bias, discrimination, and social injustice associated with past schooling practices. It utilized outcomes-based education (OBE) and called for learner-centered classrooms that promote active engagement and the development of problem-solving skills and critical and creative thinking in place of rote learning and authoritarianism, which was the norm. Revised National Curriculum Statements were released in 2001 to streamline and clarify Curriculum 2005.

The language around education reform in South Africa since 1994 has broadly and specifically appealed to democratic principles, and many of the educational changes that have been put in place have at their core the goal of building a democracy and promoting democratic principles. The South African National Curriculum Statements position education as a force that could promote values such as non-racism and reconciliation. The following statement from the National Curriculum Statement in Physical Science exemplifies the connection that is envisioned between the curriculum and democratic development at-large: "The kind of learner that is envisaged is one who will be imbued with the values and act in the interests of a society based on respect for democracy, equality, human dignity and social justice as promoted in the Constitution" (Department of Education, 2003, p. 5).

In addition to promoting the belief that "education needs to empower the learners for effective citizenry and individual enrichment" (Nelson Mandela Foundation, 2005, p. 14), the government has also promoted an ideology that "development and local participatory democracy are inseparable and complementary" (p. 14). The linkage between democracy, education, and development is quite explicit in many documents, as is the continuation of education's role as a supplier of the work force, albeit a new, technologically literate work force. This goal was summarized by the Nelson Mandela Foundation (2005) in saying, "the market requirements emphasize the need to empower the learners in sciences as this has a potential of improving the economy" (p. 174). However, Jansen (1998), writing about the South African curriculum, points out the problematic nature of assumptions about the relationship between curriculum and social or economic structure. He describes such claims as "at best misleading since they offer an economic development panacea to benefit those alienated from education and training under apartheid in the name of a complex curriculum reform policy" (p. 324). Further, he notes the complete lack of "evidence in almost 80 years of curriculum change literature to suggest that altering the curriculum of schools leads to or is associated with changes in national economies" (p. 324).

The trail of OBE in South Africa purportedly can be traced back to Australia and New Zealand (Jansen, 1998); however, many aspects of Curriculum 2005 also show close alignment with recent curricula from North America and Canada. OBE has been critiqued by many who point out that such top-down reforms actually undermine basic democratic principles and practices by depriving communities, schools, teachers and students of a voice in curriculum and assessment decisions (e.g., Portelli & Solomon, 2001). To Foucault (1977) such practices are instruments of power and domination rather than liberation, although they are often associated with education that is considered progressive, emancipatory, and democratizing. Thus, there may be inherent contradictions between the OBE approach and its democratic intentions. Complicating those contradictions further, there are also questions about the suitability of OBE for South Africa, in particular.

In the South African context, where rote learning and corporal punishment were the norm, OBE and Curriculum 2005 represent "a leap of staggering proportions" and necessitate "dramatic changes in social relations in the classroom" (Jansen, 1998, p. 325). However, despite OBE and other reforms, it is clear that a deep gap remains between "well-functioning and provisioned classrooms (predominantly housing White teachers and White or mixed classes in urban areas) and not well-functioning and poorly provisioned classrooms (largely African teachers and African pupils in peri-urban and rural areas)" (Howie & Scherman, 2008, p. 118). In my visits to rural schools in KwaZulu-Natal province in July and August of 2008 and 2009, I saw schools still struggling to recover from the material and psychological deprivation of the apartheid era and no positive signs of change stemming from OBE were evident. The post-apartheid clamor to use English as the language of instruction and assessment, the lack of teachers qualified to teach an outcome-based curriculum and to teach in English, the lack of equipment to do the types of learner-centered activities expected in the new curriculum, and the prevalence of poverty, violence, and HIV/AIDS in rural areas all mediate the implementation of the curriculum. Consequently, the divide may be widening between what is happening in relatively well resourced, well staffed, predominantly white or diverse schools in urban areas and the near destitute rural schools serving African students. With this in mind, one can recognize the emergence of exclusive forms of science from which many students continue to be marginalized.

In this period of great transition and in the midst of what may be considered the failed implementation of Curriculum 2005 in rural South African schools, teachers arrive at rural schools each day, pre-service teachers learn to teach, and teacher education programs graduate new cohorts of teachers each year. The remainder of this chapter will focus on a project intended to increase and improve the pool of teachers available to rural schools and on one science student teacher who worked in small ways to reshape his own and his students' visions and expectations about engagement in science. He exemplifies the idea that "engagement is generated through the interactions of students and teachers, in a shared space, for the purpose of democratic reconstruction, through which personal transformation takes place" (McMahon & Portelli, 2004, p. 70).

RURAL TEACHER EDUCATION PROJECT

Vulindlela is a rural area in KwaZulu-Natal about 150 kilometers from Durban and has a population of approximately 400,000. A report issued in 2005 describes the daily difficulties that the people of rural KwaZulu-Natal experience. The title of the report includes the words poverty, inequality, and unemployment (PROVIDE, 2005). In addition, Vulindlela is an area in crisis with regard to the HIV epidemic. For example, 27% of women 19 years of age or younger and about 55 percent of women ages 20 to 24 are infected (Kharsany, Carrara, Frohlich, Abdool Karim & Abdool Karim, 2005).

The Rural Teacher Education Project (RTEP) is based out of the University of KwaZulu-Natal's teacher education program at its Edgewood campus outside of Durban. Its goals are multiple. They include understanding what it means to teach in rural South African schools in the age of HIV/AIDS and how we can better prepare teachers in rural schools to work within a context of poverty and gender violence as well as AIDS. The need for teachers in rural schools in South Africa is dire. Dean Michael Samuel of the Faculty of Education described it this way to a group of student teachers: "The future of South Africa lies in what happens in rural schools in the next 20 years" (personal communication).

Beginning in July of 2007, approximately 20 students each year,[3] mainly from urban areas around Durban, did their third or fourth year teaching practicum in a rural area of KwaZulu-Natal. The district is called Vulindlela and is not quite two hours west of Durban, up toward the Drakensberg Mountains and the border of Lesotho. The student teachers lived together as a cohort, shuttling back into Durban on weekends to be with their families. During the week, they taught at one of two large secondary schools (Kuhlekonke High School and Gobindlovu High School) in the area. In 2008 and 2009, I was the on-site coordinator of the project. Working with several graduate student interns, we drove the vans full of student teachers, facilitated relations at the two schools, provided guidance and feedback to the student teachers, and ran the debriefing sessions that preceded dinner most nights.

The school discussed in this chapter is Kuhlekonke High School, which serves about 800 students, all of whom are African and speak isiZulu.[4] Many students walk long distances to and from school each day, either on dirt roads or across fields that are hot in summer and frosty in winter. The school consists of four parallel concrete buildings with classrooms that open directly to the outside. Two small additional buildings hold the administrative offices and several teacher work-rooms. None of the buildings are heated, even though the July and August winter temperatures are at times just slightly above freezing. Only the administrative building has electrical power. In the recent past, all the other buildings had electricity, but sections of the underground cables had been dug up and stolen. Many of the school's classrooms have been stripped of lighting fixtures and door locks; many windows, desks, and chalkboards are broken or damaged; and the science lab is missing all the faucets and valves that had been there just a few years before.[5] The only resources available for teaching in any subject are incomplete sets of text-books and examination guides from the Department of Education.

Most of the 14 teachers at the school arrive each day in shared taxis from two larger towns in the area; a few drive their own cars; and only two live in the town where the school is located. All are Zulu and isiZulu is their first language. They speak English with varying levels of fluency, but few feel comfortable conducting an entire class in English, despite the expectation that they would teach in English and the fact that the learners would take their matriculation exams in English.

WALLS OF SILENCE

Clark and Linder (2006) document one science teacher's efforts in post-apartheid South Africa to implement an OBE science curriculum at a school not unlike Kuhlekonke High School. They describe students as being experts at "the art of hiding," withdrawing behind "curtain walls of silence," and wearing "cloaks of anonymity" (p. 81–83). Such images portray learners as passive, almost never speaking out, and disengaged but not disruptive in the classroom. This generally concurs with what I observed in Kuhlekonke High School, where Zulu in-service and pre-service (both Zulu and white) teachers were all relatively unsuccessful in engaging students in discussions or actively involving them in learning in other ways. Clark and Cinder provided an analysis of the root of these patterns. Their argument can be summarized as attributing student passivity to factors such as large class size; learner discomfort using the medium of a second language; the historic and current use of corporal punishment; deference to the teacher's authority; a collective concept of self; a utilitarian view of schooling; and legacies of colonial oppression. Inasmuch as learners are "bound by scripts of non-participation" (Clark & Linder, 2006, p. 85), both the enactment of OBE as envisioned in Curriculum 2005 and the National Curriculum Standards and the promotion of democratic participation in classrooms is very problematic. In addition, general schooling practices have done little to alter these patterns.

So we are compelled to ask what a teacher can do in this geo-socio-political context to promote different forms of participation, what shape those new participatory practices might take, and lastly, what difference they might make to the youth of rural KwaZulu-Natal.

ONE TEACHER'S EFFORTS TO BREAK DOWN THE WALLS OF SILENCE

The tendency for learners not to participate actively in class discussions and other activities in South African classrooms has been described in many accounts, and I witnessed it in the time I spent in classrooms at two secondary schools in KwaZulu-Natal. Despite this pattern, Msizi[6], a young pre-service teacher found ways to break through the "curtain walls of silence" and create greater participation and engagement among learners in his science classroom. The students in his 9th grade physical science class participated in ways not seen in any of the other classrooms I visited and not described in the literature. They responded to his questions at times in unison and at other times individually, raised questions themselves, and contributed to discussions of science topics.

Msizi was one of the RTEP participants in 2008. He was in his mid-20s, in the fourth year of his education degree, and was doing his final practicum at Kuhlekonke High School. He had been in RTEP the year before and was previously assigned to the other secondary school that is part of the project. Msizi was a Zulu student who grew up in Durban where he attended racially mixed urban schools. His understanding and use of English were very good as was his science content knowledge. Msizi had experience as a debater and his oral abilities were excellent, including very clear enunciation and animated use of vocal inflections, skills that served him and his learners well in negotiating the language gap in the classroom.

While part of RTEP, I had the opportunity to visit Msizi's class on several occasions. The examples described here are drawn from a single class session that was videotaped. It occurred during the third week of his four-week practicum, and it was the second lesson on static electricity. The previous class included activities with balloons and pieces of paper being attracted to a charged ruler. Kuhlekonke High School in which Msizi was teaching had no science lab equipment, so we borrowed some materials, including five electroscopes, from the University of KwaZulu-Natal before going to Vulindlela. The lesson proceeded in this way:

1. Review of class rules
2. Definition of word static (not moving)
3. Review of sub-atomic particles and their charges
4. Activity with electroscopes done in small groups with discussion
5. Group reporting – "Tell what you saw and why it happened."
6. General discussion/explanation
7. Learner questions

Rather than provide learners with an initial explanation of how an electroscope works, Msizi first gave the learners experience with the electroscope on which they could build their understanding. As we look at the practices and interactions on that day, we see that, even as a new science teacher, Msizi seemed to break through the "curtain walls of silence" in his classroom and to create an ethos different from other South African classrooms. I have grouped his practices into four broad areas: language strategies; explicit teaching of norms for participation; communicating his expectation that all learners will participate; and creating cultural congruence.

MSIZI'S LANGUAGE STRATEGIES

South Africa has 11 official languages recognized in the Constitution of 1996, including nine African languages plus English and Afrikaans. The current policy is to promote additive bilingualism, but School Governing Boards can decide on the language of teaching and learning. Despite this multilingual policy, most African schools have selected English as the language of instruction. It is well documented that learners in South African schools (especially rural Black schools) "do not have the necessary English proficiency to successfully engage with the curriculum" (Probyn, 2006, p. 391), and in rural areas, they have little access to development of English proficiency.

Msizi was a fluent speaker of both English and isiZulu, the first language of all of the learners in his classroom. However, this was not the case for the learners in his classroom. Responding to the learners' needs, Msizi employed a wide array of strategies that have been identified in the literature as sound ESL strategies. For example, Msizi's reliance on repetition in his teaching can hardly be overstated. Although learners had been introduced to static electricity in previous lessons, he repeated important terms such as electron and proton numerous times in the course of the hour-long class, as shown in the transcript that follows.

At this point in the class, the learners had recalled the names of the three sub-atomic particles that they already learned (electron, proton, and neutron), and these had been listed on the board. The repetitions of <u>electron</u> are underlined for the reader.

Time since start of lesson (Min:sec)	Msizi's words	Actions
5:52	These are the very important particles when it comes to static electricity.	
5:59	But now, let us go step by step. OK, we'll start with <u>electron</u>.	
6:05	How can we define an <u>electron</u>?	A few learners raised their hands to answer the question.
6:07	What is an <u>electron</u>?	
6:09	<u>Electron.</u>	
6:11	<u>Electron.</u>	More hands are raised
6:13	What is an <u>electron</u>?	
6:15	Yes, they are all important in the static electricity.	
6:18	But now if we look at an <u>electron</u>. What is it? An <u>electron</u>.	
6:23	Yes?	Pointed to a learner who has hand raised.

Msizi repeated both the term, electron, (8 times in approximately 30 seconds) and the question. While doing this, he paused between words and phrases, actively moved throughout the room, gestured with his hands for emphasis, and used great vocal animation with rising and falling pitch and volume as he spoke. Following his initial question at 6:06, learners began to raise their hands and continued to do so until 6:23 when Msizi called on a learner. Following the learner's response, which was verified by the other learners ("Do we all agree?"), Msizi affirmed the idea that electrons have a negative charge by using the term <u>negative</u> eight times in the next 30 seconds before moving on to the next particle, proton. This is the pattern seen throughout the lesson as Msizi used repetition both of single terms and questions along with high levels of physical movement (hands and body placement) and vocal animation to encourage attention and participation by the learners.

It has been documented by numerous studies that learners in South African schools who are in classrooms where the language of instruction is not their home language often report that they do not understand what their teachers are saying (Nelson Mandela Foundation, 2005). It has also been reported (Probyn, 2006), and I have witnessed in the two schools in which RTEP was centered, that teachers in rural schools, who share a first language with the learners, often carry out instruction in their first language. This was evident at Kuhlekonke High School where many Zulu teachers resorted to oral instruction in isiZulu, although they were supposed to be teaching in English. However, Msizi retained the use of English but incorporated appropriate ESL strategies while teaching science content. These practices seemed to promote vocabulary acquisition, which is vital for oral sense-making to occur. For example, later in the lesson when students shared their ideas and asked questions, they utilized English terms such as negative effectively.

Another second language principle that Msizi exemplified was his use of the chalkboard and his body to represent scientific terms or concepts. Numerous times throughout the lesson on static electricity, Msizi drew diagrams on the board. Some of these diagrams were drawn during the explanation/discussion phase of the lesson, and others were in response to learners' questions and suggestions later in the lesson. For example, he diagrammed an electroscope as the discussion/ explanation was occurring, and he drew a representation of a charged ruler and small pieces of paper when a student asked about this activity that had been previously done. While speaking in English, he also tried to help learner understanding by acting out what he was talking about. For example, he simulated the leaves of the electroscope with outstretched arms to represent repulsion and arms hanging limply in front to represent an uncharged electroscope.

MSIZI'S EXPLICIT TEACHING OF PARTICIPATION NORMS

Since the first week, Msizi worked explicitly with the learners in the class to follow several agreed upon rules of participation. In a debriefing session with the rest of the cohort, Msizi pointed out that we cannot just assume that learners know how to participate "like we want them to" because they have never learned how to do it (Debriefing notes, August 2008).

The lesson on static electricity began with Msizi asking the learners to review the classroom rules, "Who can remind us of the first of the rules?" He utilized a repetition technique in this instance as well, asking, "How else can you define respect in the classroom?" three times and "What do you mean by respect?" two times before acknowledging a learner to give a response. After discussing the expectation to listen when someone was speaking and not to laugh at a learner's response, a learner added another rule, "You respect your teacher."

The norm of teacher respect is coherent with respect for elders, which would be expected in the community, as well as deference among African students to a teacher's authority (Shumba, 1999). However, the notion of mutual respect between teacher and learner is not common in South African schools, where learner's rights are routinely not respected (Nelson Mandela Foundation, 2005) and where many schools continue to employ corporal punishment although it has been banned. In that light, Msizi's response is unexpected and out of the ordinary.

MSIZI'S COMMUNICATION OF THE EXPECTATION THAT ALL WILL PARTICIPATE

In contrast to other classrooms, Msizi's learners were willing participants and eager to answer questions. However, as shown in the transcript that was previously discussed, Msizi did not necessarily call on the learners whose hands were first raised or with better English skills. Instead, he repeated the question until most hands in the room were raised. While doing this, he walked around and appeared to make eye contact with individual learners as if repeating the question to each of them. This approach perhaps provided even hesitant learners with time to consider their response and construct their statement in English or isiZulu. In addition, he seemed to convey the expectation that all learners would participate in valuable ways. In the length of an hour class, Msizi elicited oral involvement from almost all learners. As all classroom teachers can appreciate, this is not an easy thing to do, and it is all the more impressive in a South African classroom where learner participation is routinely minimal or non-existent.

The lack of student-initiated questions or other unsolicited contributions has been extensively described and reported in the African context (e.g., Diamondidis, 1996) and specifically in South Africa (Clark & Linder, 2006). However, in Msizi's classroom, learners not only responded individually and collectively to his questions, they also asked questions. In the second half of the class, after doing the electroscope activity and discussing what they saw, Msizi repeated questions such as "Do you understand?" and "Can you explain it now?" as he encouraged the learners to ask questions if they did not yet understand. At one point he extolled the learners saying, "You need some courage again." A learner responded in isiZulu that he did not understand. Msizi replied, "OK. Just come up with your question." The learner spoke in isiZulu for 12 seconds, using the English term negative twice in his question. Msizi responded in this way, "OK. OK. What he is basically asking is if, he says, if the ruler is negatively charged, and this electroscope is negatively charged, then how it happens." This question provided the opportunity to clarify for the class that initially the electroscope was not charged, but it became charged through induction by the negatively charged ruler.

The learners posed other "what if" and "how can that be" questions (some of which were quite lengthy) as well as queries referring back to an activity with Perspex rulers and small pieces of paper that they had done the previous day. Throughout this discussion, it is important to note that most of questions were asked in isiZulu (with some English words, mainly science terms) and were restated by Msizi in English, as shown above.

By employing language strategies that helped mitigate some of the difficulties of second language understanding and other practices that explicitly and implicitly promoted student engagement, Msizi made it more difficult for students to hide behind their "cloaks of anonymity" (Clark & Linder, 2006, p. 81). One additional approach that he took was the use of cultural congruence in his classroom.

MSIZI'S USE OF CULTURAL CONGRUENCE

The democratic project of South Africa extols multiculturalism, and Curriculum 2005 and the National Curriculum Standards advise teachers to link teaching and learning with the learners' culture.[7] However, examples or materials illustrating how to create such cultural congruence and inclusion are not provided to teachers.

Although Msizi is Zulu, he grew up in an urban setting where, according to him, being Zulu meant something different than it does in the rural area of Vulindlela. His knowledge of the local context, which might have allowed him to connect science with practices such as agriculture or medicine, was limited. However, when possible he used examples from learners' lives to explain or help students visualize things. For example, in contrasting electric currents that flow with static electricity, he referred to the large electrical transmission lines that crisscrossed the surrounding hills and under which many learners walked to school. He also referred to the lack of electrical power in the majority of the school, which was caused by intruders to the school grounds digging up and stealing the large underground cable delivering power to the classrooms. When teaching the learners that a negative sign represents an electron and a positive sign represents a proton, Msizi preceded that with the following example of how we use symbols as shorthand representations.

> In most cases when you talk about HIV and AIDS, we normally use a symbol, a special symbol that symbolizes HIV or AIDS. So in most cases when you see that symbol, you know that that's the sign for HIV and AIDS. The same thing applies to the first two particles.

Learners at Kuhlekonke High School come face to face with HIV/AIDS daily in their families, schools, and community. Msizi's use of these examples illustrate how, albeit in limited ways, he responded to the lack of culturally congruent science resources by drawing on these very obvious artifacts to contextualize his science teaching.

Msizi frequently used call and response patterns, which are characteristic of many Sub-Saharan cultures. Smitherman (1977) defines call and response as "spontaneous verbal and non-verbal interaction between speaker and listener in which all of the statements ('calls') are punctuated by expressions ('responses') from the listener" (p. 104). In call and response there is usually an initiator (in this case, Msizi) and multiple responders (the learners). As shown in Table 6.1, several types of call and response patterns were evident during the static electricity lesson.

Msizi's use of call and response in his science teaching can be understood as culturally congruent and thus potentially contributing to the unique participation patterns that he was able to foster. The role of teacher as initiator is aligned with learner expectations of the teacher as an authority figure, making this form of participation more likely to strike a chord of cultural resonance with the learners. In some usages, call and response is very spontaneous and can be described as a cultural form of democratic participation. Msizi's class does not represent this liberatory expression of call and response inasmuch as the participants' efforts are mediated by the post-apartheid context. Although Msizi did not share all aspects

Table 6.1. Call and response patterns

Call and response type		Initiator (Msizi)	Responders (learners, in unison)
Neighboring	Responders repeat the phrase	Electron. Can you all say that?	Electron
Ellipsing	Responders complete the initiator's sentence	The teacher as well should respect↑	Learners
Closed inquiry	Initiator asks a question that elicits a simple, often one-word response	She says an electron has a negative charge. Do we all agree?	Yes

of Zulu culture and experiences with his students, he relied on those that they did share in the form of patterns of oral participation and used those to penetrate the passivity of his students to some extent.

WHAT CAN BE LEARNED FROM MSIZI'S CLASS?

Many times during my work with the Rural Teacher Education Project, I realized that I did not know the culture of the learners, school, and community sufficiently to give specific advice on how to teach in Vulindlela, South Africa. However, my perspective as a teacher educator and a science educator enabled me to recognize instances of difference, that is, those times when the boundaries were stretched beyond the status quo and when new visions emerged of what a rural science class-room could be like in South Africa. And I could help the other teachers learn from those occurrences and share those glimpses with others through this chapter.

Democratic science education can be envisioned as bottom-up science that emanates from the lives of the learners. Elsewhere, I have referred to this as emergent science (Seiler, 2001), and it necessitates new forms of participation by teachers and students. Though the goal is an important one, fostering new patterns of science participation among populations that have been marginalized in school and science is no easy task. (Seiler and Gonsalves, in press). Democratic, transformative intentions often collide with the norms and practices of non-participation to which learners have been socialized. Using a Marxist lens, Martin (2008, p. 32) describes this alienation in American schools as a "culture of sabotage," but it seems similar to the "curtain walls of silence" described for South African schools. Inasmuch as Msizi's students participated in ways uncommon in other rural South African class-rooms, there is something to be learned from his science classroom.

North American readers may see Msizi's classroom as falling short of participatory democracy in many ways. The learners raised their hands to be acknowledged by the teacher, much of the hour was quite teacher-centered, the teacher asked most of the questions, and the topic itself was selected by the teacher to align with the National Curriculum Standards. Some types of participation accomplished by Msizi relied on cued elicitation and may not lead to real understanding of the science content (Clark & Linder, 2006). However, to take only this view would ignore the small but very significant steps that this classroom made toward a different ethos of participation than remains the norm in rural, South African schools. The learners responded more (both individually and collectively) than in most classrooms. They worked in groups with the electroscopes and carried out independent discussions that included attempts to make sense of what they observed. They switched between isiZulu and English as they appropriated science vocabulary. Later in the lesson, learners asked questions themselves, in marked contrast with the science classroom reported by Clark & Linder and many others who have documented South African classrooms where learner-initiated interactions almost never occur. Although Msizi did maintain the lead in the lesson, he explicitly and implicitly worked to establish new norms of participation and deftly used ways of participating that were familiar to the learners (e.g., call and response) to actively engage the learners. He took the geo-socio-cultural context of rural South Africa into account and found some starting points for science education to become transformative, at least of individuals. As LeGrange (2007) suggests for South African education during this difficult transition, Msizi focused on the language of probability instead of the language of possibility.

Msizi's class also reminds us that our expectations of what student-centered learning and participatory democracy in a classroom might look like are culturally shaped. Thus, we must question the nature of democratic expectations that come in the form of top-down policies such as curriculum documents influenced by educational approaches and ideologies from other places. We must consider the cultural congruence and appropriateness of them in places shaped by and recovering from colonial oppression.

Working within the structural constraints of English as the language of instruction, lack of resources, effects of rurality (poverty, violence, and HIV/AIDS), the impending lack of employment opportunities for the learners, and the legacy of ineffective and authoritarian schooling, a young teacher was able to use his own and borrowed resources to foster unexpected levels of science participation and engagement. His classroom perhaps illustrates that some possibilities exist for the development of a culture of human rights and democracy in classrooms in South Africa, but they require new relationships between teachers and learners that will not happen overnight. It remains to be seen what those new relationships will look like and how they might shape or mirror social transformation throughout South Africa. Msizi drew upon and yet pushed classroom norms and ways of being in rural KwaZulu-Natal. In doing so, he created a classroom that was aligned in some small way with Jhumki's vision in that it "reflect[ed] the beliefs, ideas and creativity of the teachers and students" (Basu, this volume). And I might add "hopes" to that list.

NOTES

[1] The education system in South Africa uses the term *learner* in place of *student* or *pupil*. It's use represents the learner-centered education called for in the new curriculum.

[2] In rural South Africa, conditions of poverty and health prevent many children from participating successfully in education or attending school regularly. Not diminishing the complex interplay between education and out-of-school contexts, this chapter looks closely at what happened inside one rural science classroom.

[3] In 2008, there were 12 Zulu and 8 white pre-service teachers; in 2009 there were 19 Zulu and 1 white pre-service teachers.

[4] isiZulu is the language of the Zulu people.

[5] Although all schools in the area were at risk for vandalism and theft, Kuhlekonke High School had experienced more than most. It was difficult for the local people to pinpoint the cause of this destruction to the school infrastructure. Generally it was attributed to bad relations between the school principal and the community coupled with the lack of a 24-hour watch at the school and openings in the barbed wire fence that surrounded the grounds.

[6] A pseudonym is used for the teacher.

[7] Much has been written about the incorporation of indigenous knowledge into science teaching, and some learning outcomes in the South African National Curriculum Standards focus on rediscovering indigenous scientific knowledge. However, a review of that literature is beyond the scope and intent of this chapter.

CHRISTOPHER EMDIN

7. CITIZENSHIP AND THE THREE C'S

Cogenerative Dialogues, Coteaching and Cosmopolitanism

The underlying premise of this chapter is that social injustice in the world beyond
the classroom is a significant component of the student experiences in schools, and
affects what goes on within the classroom (Hacker 1995, DeCruir & Dixson, 2007).
The permeation of these inequities through the membranes of safe spaces like
schools, has deep sociopsychological effects on students (Williams, 1999), and creates
a general disadvantage for students of color (Kao & Thompson, 2006). The result
of these disadvantages is that populations who have been victimized by social
injustice in spaces beyond the classroom are often ill prepared to be full participants
within the urban science classroom.

The actions and behaviors that signify the permeation of social injustices beyond
the classroom into the classroom are often enacted or replicated by teachers and
other structures within science classrooms (Bryan & Atwater, 2002). The enactment
of practices that are reminiscent of socially unjust spaces, or that consciously
or unconsciously function to, create inequitable spaces within classrooms, inhibits
students from being full participants in the urban science classroom. Even when
individuals think, act, and vote to get what they want in traditionally democratic
institutions, the democratic values of participation and fairness are under-focused
upon (Fung, 2004). This is particularly the case in the physics classroom where
"despite considerable evidence that traditional approaches are ineffective in teaching
physics concepts, most physics students in this country continue to be taught in
lectures and assessed individually (Thorton and Sokoloff, 1997). Furthermore,
solutions to problems are often formula based and focused on an individual students'
determination of an unknown quantity in provided questions (Van Heuvelen, 1991).
Physics classrooms look the same, and students are underprepared for working with
each other despite research that indicates that collaborative learning is a necessary
approach to instruction. Lemke (2000) reminds us that even in "democratic" classrooms, students are trained to be autonomous. Autonomy in the classroom – whether
it be implicitly or explicitly approved – undermines fairness because it presents
opportunities to reflect or deliberate on what it means to be a full participant in the
science classroom.

The first goal of this chapter is to present a newly emerging framework for
conducting research that focuses on social justice in urban science classrooms. The
second is to use this framework as a means for addressing these social justice
issues in the classroom. I use the three C's as a means to both collect data and

*S.J. Basu et al., (eds.), Democratic Science Teaching: Building the Expertise to Empower
Low-Income Minority Youth in Science, 103–114*

provide a framework for research designed to optimize participant involvement in the urban science classroom. When the three C's merge with the concept of citizenship, the culturalizing process (Parsons, 2000) is enacted, and a path towards equity and fairness as they relate to the students' experience in the classroom is presented.

CITIZENSHIP

The overarching framework for addressing the injustices in the science classroom is the concept of citizenship. The United States Constitution describes citizenship as a process where privileges or immunities of all people who are considered citizens are undeniable (U.S Constitution). However, as is the case when we describe the phrase "all", as in "science for all" or "citizenship for all", realities of racial, ethnic and linguistically diverse populations within the category of "all" are often masked. Banks (2008) discusses this caveat of citizenship when he argues that if being a citizen revolves around just being within the nation and not being involved in the social, political and civil processes within the nation, the process "result[s] in the treatment of some groups as second class citizens because [their] group rights are not recognized" (p. 131). This caveat, where a certain hierarchy exists that positions first class and second class citizens, falls in line with the flaws of multi-cultural science classrooms. Within these classrooms, "science for all" or even social justice within classrooms may not be effective because an existent slogan or law about citizenship, justice, or multiculturalism cannot control deficit-laden perspectives about the value and worth of others. Furthermore, multicultural movements that do not fully emphasize issues related to everyday injustices such as the inability of certain groups to fully participate in the classroom will function to maintain the status quo (Speight, 2000). As Lipman (2004) suggests, when there is a steady flow of immigrants into urban areas, an ever-evolving politics of race, class and diversity is created where a new group is always available to be viewed as a partial participant in society. In urban classrooms, this dynamic is inherited and certain students are treated like partial participants.

Full participation and citizenship in the classroom are indelibly linked. By full participation, I argue for moving beyond a superficial involvement in the classroom such as responding to a question or raising one's hand to get the teachers attention as participation (Kress, Jewitt & Ogborne, 2001). Full participation involves all of the teaching and learning processes in the classroom, such as lesson planning, coteaching, discussing the classroom, and developing instructional approaches with the teacher. Additionally, full participation in the classroom for all students is an avenue through which students may have greater opportunities to feel like citizens of the classroom and social justice is attained. Full participation, which provides multiple avenues for students to connect to the classroom, is an integral component of "culturalizing" that is necessary in the urban science classroom. The lack of consideration for the role of cultural differences as they play out within different classrooms, is the chief inhibitor to the attainment of social justice (Goodman, 2001). When all students in the classroom are for the most part, evenly culturalized into the classroom, then they can be all viewed as citizens of the classroom.

Banks' (2008) discussion on three strands of citizenship—civil, political, and social that were first explicated by Marshall (1964)—help to further unpack the relationship between full participation and citizenship. These strands are beneficial for addressing social injustice within urban science classrooms because they can serve as a pathway to providing social justice to marginalized groups. For example, the granting of civil citizenship to women through the call for women's right to vote, and the subsequent granting of political citizenship through the passing of the nineteenth amendment did not inhibit sexism and the social ostracization of outspoken women leaders. Furthermore, attempts at social and civil citizenship for African Americans in the late 1780's could never be achieved when political citizenship was denied by the three-fifths compromise. The point here is that inequities, without addressing the power structures that cause them, such as deep seated bias, or the blind repetition of existent practice develops into passivity in fighting oppression, allows for people to be only partial citizens in society.

However, we face a situation, where, traditionally, students are not provided the tools to be more active citizens that advocate for themselves (O'Donoghue, Krishner and McLaughlin, 2002). This process requires moving beyond the existent model of participation in the classroom where the teacher picks students to answer questions or have certain roles in the classroom, and moving towards a model where students have the tools to create spaces for themselves in the classroom, discuss the inhibitors to their success, and address these issues. This is where I believe that the 3 C's for Urban Science Education become beneficial, because they stand as a triad of tools that students can use to provide each other with opportunities for fairness, equity and full participation.

THE THREE C'S FOR URBAN SCIENCE EDUCATION

The three C's can be used to both theorize and create practices that could be implemented in the classroom. Here, they are utilized as a means to possibly ameliorate the situations where certain students are denied full participation or citizenship in science and/or the science classroom. Individually, each of the 3C's addresses a specific strand of citizenship (civil, political and social). As a triad of tools, they provide an opportunity for the science educator to provide a set of collective steps that can give students opportunities for full participation in the classroom and consequently, provide opportunities for social justice.

Viewing full participation as citizenship in the classroom, and using the three 3C's to reach this goal, is not only a means through which social justice is addressed in the classroom, but a necessary supplement to existent approaches to instruction that focus on the consideration of the contexts beyond the classroom in the delivery of science instruction. The 3C's also have a significant purpose in the argument for social justice because they are not only tools for citizenship in the science classroom, but are also essential tools for implementing what other researchers in social justice work have articulated as the goals of their work. For example, the five dimensions of multicultural education articulated by Cochran-Smith (2004), can be achieved through the 3 C's. These dimensions, which include using content from diverse groups in classroom instruction, helping students understand how knowledge is constructed, helping students develop positive inter-group attributes, helping them develop positive inter-group behaviors, and modifying teaching in ways that meet students' needs are often articulated without the provision of a plan for implementing them. Therefore, in the paragraphs that follow, I elaborate on each of the three C's and discuss how they can be implemented within urban science classrooms to achieve social justice.

Cogenerative Dialogues

Cogenerative dialogues (cogens) are when students and teachers have joint conversations about their experiences inside and outside of classrooms, with the goal of reaching collective decisions about the rules, roles, and responsibilities that govern their lives (Roth et al., 2002). Beginning with a few students and a teacher, and focusing on a science class that they all are a part of, teachers and students through discussion try to decide upon at least one thing that the group can do to improve the science classroom. This strand of the 3 C's helps students to develop positive inter-group attributes, and positive inter-group behaviors because they are connected in social spaces where the goal is for them to interact.

Ideally, cogens occur with 4–6 participants who represent different groups in the classroom. The participants may be high and low achievers, students who both participate in the classroom and do not, or students from different ethnic or racial backgrounds. Because cogens ideally function with a small group that represents the different constituencies in the classroom, they are likely to be focused on specific issues that a student or group of students may have, and the creation of a possible solution to these issues. In the cogens, students are invited to participate but can always opt out of engaging in future dialogues. This process functions to create the space for urban students from various ethnic backgrounds to develop intergroup attitudes and behaviors.

Once consistent dialogues are in place, there are certain rules that are set in place so that they can run properly. The first is that all participants in the dialogues have equal turns at talk. All participants, including teachers agree to not monopolize conversations. The second rule is that all participants within the dialogue engage in talk that is respectful of other participants. All participants are asked to listen attentively and allow their peers to complete their thoughts before responding. The third rule is that a plan of action for addressing issues raised in dialogues must be generated from the conversation and implemented in future classes. Throughout this process, students are able to become involved as researchers and practitioners in the teaching and learning of science in the classroom (LaVan & Beers, 2005). They are also able to provide feedback to teachers about ways to improve instruction, and able to see plans of action that they suggest in dialogues become implemented in the classroom. These dialogues function to provide full participation/citizenship by providing civil citizenship in the classroom through their provision of opportunities for cordial interactions among participants.

Coteaching

Coteaching, another strand of the 3 C's, supports full participation in the science classroom by allowing the student to take on the role of teacher. Usually students coteach on the topics and ideas that come up in the cogens, furthering their agency. Furthermore, coteaching supports positive inter-group attributes, helps student develop positive inter-group behaviors, and works towards modifying teaching in ways that meet students' needs by placing the student in front of the classroom and assisting them in communicating with peers from different backgrounds.

In traditional versions of coteaching, the perception is that interprofessional collaboration amongst teachers contributes to meeting the needs of children (Kenny et al., 2007). Coteaching, as used in this study, and when enacted alongside cogens, extends beyond this assertion by positioning students as the professionals in the distinct domains that affect their lives. Students become teachers – the ones who are responsible for their peers, and the ones who make the decisions about what is effective in the teaching and learning process. This take on coteaching varies from conventional forms where the professionals are teachers at different stages of their career (Roth et al., 2002) or from different disciplines like a content area and special education (Reinhiller, 1996).

Coteaching provides students with opportunities to disclose their strengths and/or weaknesses in regards to the science content and share their general comfort or discomfort with particular topics. For example, in enacting coteaching, students can co-plan with the teacher, review the topic that will be taught in class, collectively decide on assignments, and then teach lesson to their peers. These practices are designed to create opportunities for students to become active participants in the classroom. It also gives them the opportunities to both seek and exercise power in the affairs of the classroom, and actively work towards being more active participants. This process of seeking and exercising power that coteaching provides goes hand in hand with political citizenship because it is designed to allow a student to become more of an active participant in the inner workings of the classroom.

Cosmopolitanism

Cosmopolitanism is a philosophical understanding that focuses on the notion that all of humanity are citizens of the world, and that each person has a responsibility for ensuring that all people are treated equally (Appiah, 2006). While cogens more broadly focus on developing plans of action for improving the classroom, and coteaching involves the expansion of the role of the student to include that of teacher, cosmopolitanism is the focus on developing deep connections with students across racial, ethnic, linguist and gender differences so that they can get the most out of the classroom. It is the set of processes that are enacted that help students to feel like they are citizens of the classroom that is enacted by purposefully identifying and replicating processes that allow all students to be responsible for each others' teaching and learning. Cosmopolitanism is marked by instances where students begin to engage in their own cogens and coteaching without prompts from the teacher. I believe that social citizenship is made possible through a cosmopolitan orientation in the classroom. When students and the teacher pay close attention to, and take every opportunity to, ensure that everyone is connected to teaching and learning in the classroom, then new spaces of interaction are supported, allowing students to seek the companionship of others and see the value in learning about the thoughts, ideas and contributions of others. Furthermore, social citizenship extends into civil and political citizenship when there is a true desire to connect to others and learn more about who they are, and how and why knowledge about who they are can benefit everyone in the science classroom.

LEARNING IN URBAN CLASSROOMS

I carried out my work in a ninth grade physics classroom within an urban public school in a major Northeastern city in the United States. Students in the science classroom were asked to volunteer to be participants in the study and were permitted to invite their peers. In the school, 98% of the students qualify for free and/or reduced lunch and 99% of the students are classified as African-American and Hispanic. While the students in the classroom were classified as either African American or Hispanic according to the school data, many of them classified themselves as having hyphenated American identities such as Dominican-American, Mexican-American, or Jamaican-American. While cogens were held with all students in the class based on random groupings, students who had volunteered, who represented each of the various ethnic backgrounds in the classroom were invited to be a part of a particular set of weekly dialogues. Even though students were only in cogens in groups of four to six at a time during lunch, and occasionally after school, all students out of the 27 in the class were either involved in cogens, or coteaching at some point during the academic year.

In my classroom, the 3C Citizenship approach seemed to challenge assumptions (and associated practices) in the classroom about who could do science. Further the approach also supported teachers and students in uncovering how unfair assumptions often led to classroom practices that fostered social injustice. Additionally, by allowing for explicit affirmation of diversity and the role of diversity in uncovering inequitable practices, the 3C Citizenship model also fostered an increase in student participation and performance. Much of this increased participation can be traced back to what I refer to as "collective frustration" however, it could also be traced back to the participation structures put into play by the 3C Citizenship model. I discuss these points below.

Challenging Assumptions

One of the ways in which social injustice played out in the physics class was by the practices which privileged some students over others in terms of access to science. A clear and consistent practice related to the distribution of material resources. As is typical in many urban high schools, the material resources, such as text books and lab equipment, in 9th grade physics were limited, and students were often expected to share them. Yet, how the students enacted the meaning of shared materials fostered assumptions about who had the right materials and what that meant for who had the right to do science. For example, I noted that time and time again when students were deprived of science materials or books, there was a general class consensus that those who did not get the materials did not have the right or privilege to do science. Neither did those not granted materials ask for them nor did those students granted the materials offer to share. However, this often led to tensions as those students without materials often resisted classroom activity when they did not have materials. For example, VTR analysis that showed students from the left side of the room attempting to make objections to being denied materials in the beginning of the year, and their non-response to being denied materials as the year progressed. Jose, for example, raises this point when he says in response to a student who said "he couldn't use the materials anyway": "After a while, when I was just shut down and couldn't even talk in class, I started asking myself if I was really dumb or something." This quote shows that some of the students internalized this lack of access as a reflection on their abilities. Cogens, which allowed the students the space to talk about these feelings, allowed these assumptions to surface and be challenged.

What also contributed to the tensions in the class was that who had access (and who did not) affected the students in the class differentially. The main victims of this form of social injustice were most often the Latino/a immigrant students. I purpose-fully use the term victim to indicate that not only were these students recipients of limited resources, they were also subject to other classroom practices which limited their full participation, such as being interrupted when they spoke, being teased because of their accents, and having materials taken from them on a regular basis. VTR analysis, when combined with interviews, revealed that these injustices were not necessarily rooted in classroom practice, but in longer-term social histories outside of school. The students who were victims mentioned that they were described by as "new to the hood" or "fresh off the boat" outside of the school by people other than their peers as well. Through studies of VTR to identify certain students, and subsequent interviews with them, it became clear that African-American and Puerto-Rican students, who were in the neighborhood the longest had similar accents. In another study related to hip-hop and science, they revealed that they listened to the same music. These students were the primarily the ones who victimized their new immigrant peers. When they were with their new immigrant peers, they would talk about their connections to each other that the new immigrants did not know.

For example, in one cogen, students who were from the middle table or the tables on the right side of the room would mention the Northeast blackout of 2003 and the neighborhood barbecues, search for radios, and impromptu parties that they experienced. They continued these discussions even though their peers who had not experienced this event did not know what they were talking about. One student mentioned to a new immigrant peer that, "You wouldn't understand you were probably on a boat or something when that happened." When this type of statement was made, as the researcher, I referred to being a "good citizen" in order to remind students that it was necessary to maintain fairness in the classroom but also to open up dialog across these differences.

Once students who worked to exclude their peers and those who were excluded were engaged in the 3C's together, they worked with each other in the planning phases of coteaching, they reported that they spoke to each other outside of the classroom when they rarely did before, and they discussed issues that were beyond the classroom such as ethnic and racial misconceptions and racism. One significant issue that emerged from their newfound collaborations was their collective frustration with learning certain physics topics.

Explicit Attention to Diversity

Cogens and coteaching also surfaced attention to the fact that many divisions across ethnic boundaries existed in the classroom, and that these divisions had a direct implication on whether or not certain students had the opportunity to actively participate in science or be citizens of the classroom. Because the school prohibited assigned seating in the classroom, students could sit wherever they felt most comfortable. VTRs of the classroom showed distinct ethnicity based seating arrangements in the physics class. Puerto Rican and African-American students sat at two different tables on one side of the room, and Dominican-American and Mexican-American students sat on the other side of the classroom. At the back of the classroom, there were three tables where Caribbean-American students sat and where other students that were of Latino decent but were not Dominican or Puerto-Rican sat. In the middle of the room, there was a mixed group of African-American and Puerto-Rican students. While these seating practices were visible to all and had come to be accepted, they were never talked about directly in terms of the racial divisions they reproduced until taken up in the cogens in the context of which side of the room "talks".

For example, the VTR revealed that students from the African-American and Puerto-Rican group in the middle of the room, and the Puerto-Rican and African-American tables on the right side of the room responded to teacher questions at least twice as often than their peers from other tables. In addition, whenever other students attempted to answer questions, their peers from the middle and right side of the room would interrupt and speak over them. One VTR of the classroom used in a cogen showed one instance where a Mexican-American student attempted to answer a teacher question about whether potential or kinetic energy was depicted in the diagram. As the student began to answer, a Puerto-Rican student interrupted and said "potential energy". When the student who was supposed to answer the question responded, he said kinetic energy; which was the right answer. As I commended him for giving the right answer, students from the Puerto-Rican and African-American tables began to make statements alluding to their perception that the Mexican American student only got the answer correctly because he guessed. One student from the middle table said, "ask us (African-American and Puerto-Rican students) another question we will get it before them (other Latino/a students). These types of scenarios led to conversations in cogens where a Columbian born student said, "all the people... we're just with their own type, and didn't (don't) care about nobody else." VTR of the classroom were also able to show that certain students were treated like second-class citizens by being prevented from fully participating in the science classroom activities and/or discussions. These students were interrupted when they spoke in class, and also those whose efforts to get materials were interrupted by their peers. For example, the class had only a set of twenty books for the close to thirty students in the classroom. However, when the textbooks were distributed, certain students who sat on the right side of the room would make sure that everyone in their groups would have a book while students from the Mexican-American or other than Puerto-Rican Latino/a group would not have any books for their entire group. This practice also happened with the distribution of materials for the creation of balloon-powered cars where students would have extra materials such as balloons, or index cards but would not share with students from certain ethnic groups. Further evidence of the divisions among students were noted in classroom VTR that showed that certain students would mimic each others accents, roll their eyes when their peers from different ethnic backgrounds were talking, and take materials from certain students' tables without permission. In one instance a student responded to a question about which of two objects the teacher was holding up would have more inertia by saying" the one with mas (more in spanish) mass, pero (because) the one with mas mass has more inertia. A student in the class responded to this answer by yelling "Mas Mas Mas Mas... nobody knows what the hell you people are talking about."

Bonding through Collective Frustration

Cogens and coteaching provided unique spaces for frustration to be not only an important but also a necessary dimension of learning to participate more fully. Frustration provided different spaces for students to expand on the political and social aspects of citizenship in the classroom. For example, in a previous lesson, different concepts and formulas related to work and force were explained to students. They all seemed to understand the lesson and were able to answer certain word problems related to calculating net force on an object when certain types of forces were applied to the object. In the lesson the next day, they were shown that there were more possible forces acting upon an object. They were then shown diagrams that depicted the types and directions of forces acting upon an object. Students were asked to indicate which force(s) are doing work upon the object, and calculate the work done by these forces. In the cogen after this lesson, An African-American student named Erin commented that, "This lesson made no sense... How do you talk about formulas one day, and then all of a sudden start drawing diagrams?" A Puerto-Rican student named Linda mentioned that "He (the teacher) is combining too many things into one topic and this is frustrating." A Dominican-American student named Carlos then responded by saying, I don't get this stuff either. "Janice, a Columbian-American student who rarely spoke in class said, "Why are we drawing in physics anyway?" Erin then responded by saying, you're right, everybody agrees, this makes no sense." These comments indicated that a number of students shared a level of frustration with learning about forces and work. This dialogue led to Jose, a previously silenced Mexican American student to mention that he "kind of understands the lesson." Jose took out a piece of paper, and then explained a word problem that was a part of the previous lesson. This question required students to calculate the force of gravity acting on a 10 gram object. Janice, responded by saying that "I know how to solve a word problem but I don't get today's lesson." As the rest of the group nodded in agreement with Janice, Jose drew a free body diagram based on the word problem that he had just solved. He then solved the same problem based on the formula for finding the force of gravity with a given mass. He talked through the steps of the problem, and then looked up when he completed it. Erin asked, "Is that the same problem?" and Jose responded by saying "Yes, its just drawing the same thing." Linda then drew a free body diagram question from the class earlier in the day that asked for net force and said "What about this?" Jose then wrote out a word problem based on the diagram and solved it. Erin responded by saying, "So that is the same problem", and proceeded to solve it on his own. He then said, "this dude is really smart and is a good teacher." As the rest of the group nodded in agreement, Linda said, "next time we have a test, I'm studying with you." Jose smiled, Carlos agreed by saying "Yes, the other side of the class knows stuff too", and the students seemed to have overcome an obstacle together.

In an interview with Jose, three days after the cogen where he got a chance to teach his peers, he said "After coteaching was the first time I really felt like a part of the classroom, I loved when they asked me questions and I could just talk to them for once." In another cogen Erin, who previously prevented other non African-American students from participating, was teaching an ethnically diverse group about Keplers Law and said "I just want to do what I can to make sure that everyone understands the formula." Erin's quote indicates that the divides that existed within the classroom were slowly being overcome through dialogues, coteaching, and the enactment of a cosmopolitan ethos among students in the classroom.

Through the research in this study, it also became apparent that "the repeated everyday experience of being treated as an inferior produces a public image of being an inferior" (Deutsch, 2006, p. 18). Once students who were previously victimized were able to teach their peers across ethnic groups, and work with them on improving the classroom in cogens, the "us" versus "them" discourse evident in how they shared resources and talked to and about each other started to shift. For example, about a week after Jose's initial breakthrough with his peers, Carlos and Linda volunteered to teach a classroom lesson on sound waves. As they taught, they were so clear in their explanations, and purposeful in asking all students to be a part of the lesson, that they set a tone that all students were accepted. Carlos asked a student from each table to solve a question, asked each group to come to the board to explain their solution, and Linda went to each group to help those who were struggling to understand the concept. Students' statements in interviews after this class indicated that they began to see formerly ostracized students as fellow citizens of the science classroom. One student, who sat at the Caribbean/African American table mentioned that "the students who usually sit on the other side of the classroom are part of us. They're just like everybody else, if we get it, we all get it, and if we don't, we all don't get it."

Changing the Dynamics of Full Participation

As student opportunities to reflect on the social injustices in science class expanded, their practices for participation in class appeared to shift in noticeable ways. For example, in addition to the above findings, the research shows that the extent to which students treated each other civilly grew with the implementation of the 3C's. Evidence of this growth in civility was captured on videotape as students interrupted their peers from different ethnic backgrounds from speaking in the class fewer times as the study progressed, worked with each other across ethnic divides to work on classroom assignments, and raised their hands to answer questions rather than blurting them out when others, who may not be as outspoken from other ethnic groups, may possibly have an answer as well. On one occasion, before a unit exam on Work, Energy, and Power, students were captured on VTR quizzing each other across ethnic groups while their peers in the cafeteria remained in their ethnically separated groups.

While one may argue that civility is a subjective feature of changing participation, I argue that it opens up new spaces for a wider range of students to participate. For example, the implementation of approaches to citizenship also led to an increase in classroom participation and performance. Evidence of this increased participation was revealed by studies of classroom VTR's both before and after the 3C's were implemented and then played out in the classroom. Students who rarely raised their hands in class or spoke during the classroom before the implementation of the approaches described in this article, began to raise their hands more often, increased discussions about science, and had increased test scores when compared to the earlier part of the academic year. Interviews with students revealed that prior to the implementation of the 3C's, many recent Latino/a and African immigrant students mentioned that they felt like they were not a part of the classroom. After its implementation, one student mentioned, "I finally feel like I count."

BUILDING JUST AND DEMOCRATIC CLASSROOMS IN URBAN SETTINGS

The research described in this chapter has been targeted specifically to urban science education because it is a means to addressing social injustice by focusing on the diverse needs of youth in urban classrooms. As the field of science education positions issues that directly relate to the urban students' experience as secondary to other foci of the discipline, revelations of the ethnic divisions in urban classrooms provided by this work threatens to hinder a large number of youth in science classrooms from doing well in science. In physics, which is a field of study that requires participation, group work, and peer instruction in order to be taught effectively (Redish et al., 1998), the absence of civility, fairness or full participation threatens effective learning of the subject matter.

Adams, Bell and Griffin (1997) discuss in their work that teaching for social justice requires both a process and a goal. Full participation, citizenship, and social justice can be seen as synonyms goals that are reached for on different levels. Full participation is what the teacher works towards, citizenship is what is held to students as an ideal, and social justice is the larger goal that both includes and goes beyond the classroom. Findings of this paper show that creating the space to address injustice in the classroom increases the participation of all students and allows for more equitable and fair practices that promote social justice.

The 3C Citizenship Model provides a way that these socially unjust and oppressive practices are targeted and addressed so that students can connect themselves to the science classroom and feel like they are a part of science. Science has often been described as a patriarchal discipline (Harding, 1993) and a space where "oppression is enacted upon the least empowered members" (Valente, 2001, p. 123). This is why the part of this study that focuses specifically on dialogues amongst students from different ethnic groups is so significant. Participation in the cogens, where no ethnic group is outnumbered, and everyone has equal voice, potentially redistributes the power dynamics in the classroom and allows the formerly powerless groups to find strength through the newfound positions as coteacher and citizen in the classroom. In essence, the study that is described in this paper can be beneficial both in its outline of an approach to addressing classroom injustice, and as an example of ways to practically enact approaches to addressing social injustice that is rooted in finding voice for marginalized youth in urban settings.

The uneven historical foundation to science, and the fact that students of color rarely see themselves as part of the discipline or the world beyond it, is itself a major issue in urban science education. However, within urban science classrooms, educators have the opportunity to position the classroom as a space where this replication of oppression through science is addressed. In so doing, students can be exposed to a new and more inclusive reality and can connect to science in profound ways. Therefore, urban science education has a major role to play in addressing social injustice and/or creating possibilities for it.

It is the responsibility of urban science education to provide urban youth with a picture of citizenship through their involvement in the science classroom that they would not get in other spaces. Through the 3C's, students are able to gain civil, political and social citizenship and develop the ability to leverage their full citizenship in the science classroom into working towards attaining social justice in their schools, and in their communities.

ANGELA CALABRESE BARTON AND EDNA TAN
(ALPHABETICAL)

8. WHY DEMOCRATIC SCIENCE
TEACHING MATTERS

"Although the largest 100 urban school districts represent less than one-tenth of 1% of the 16,850 public school districts in the United States, these districts serve nearly one-quarter (23%) of all public school students in the country. These same 100 districts also educate approximately 40% of all nonwhite students and 30% of students from low income families" (Improving Academic Achievement in Urban Districts: What State Policymakers Can Do, 2003). Yet, teacher demographics even in these large urban areas do not come close to matching the students'(Gordon, Della Piana, & Keleher, 2000). In her review on preparing teachers for culturally diverse schools, Sleeter (2001) talks of the overwhelming presence of Whiteness in preservice programs. According to NCES (2004), the enrollment in public elementary and secondary schools in 2001 was 60% White, 38% Black, 17% Hispanic, 4% Asian/Pacific Islander and 1% American Indian/Alaskan Native. In contrast, the teaching force in 2000 was 84% White, 8% Black, 6% Hispanic and 2.5% belonging to other minority groups.

These statistics point to the demographic gap between teachers and students. Yet, it is the "cultural gap" that is just as much of an issue when those interested in teaching largely live in and embody different social worlds from the students they are to teach (Ladson Billings, 1999). Several studies point towards how preservice teachers hold a deficit view of urban youth, assuming that not all students can learn, or that when students "fail" to learn it is the students fault rather than a possible problem in the processes of schooling (Goodlad, 1990). This is further supported by research findings which reveal that the widely held beliefs among preservice teachers that urban youth are somehow deficient and even deviant, in contrast to themselves. For example, according to McIntyre (1997), preservice teachers typically see themselves as "committed individuals, having good parents, good values, a good education, and a good sense of what is expected from them as teachers. In contrast they see students of color as not having – as somehow deficient" (p. 135). Schultz et al. (1996), in a survey of three hundred preservice teachers, found that they have stereotypic beliefs about urban children e.g., they believe that urban youth have attitudes that interfere with education. In this survey, the education students used words such as *unmotivated, screw-you attitude, rougher, violent, more streetwise, lackadaisical* and *emotionally unstable* to describe urban students (see also Wolffe, 1996, Terrill & Mark 2000, Lazar, 1998 & Groulx, 2001 for similar findings).

*S.J. Basu et al., (eds.), Democratic Science Teaching: Building the Expertise to Empower
Low-Income Minority Youth in Science, 115–120.*

We are left with the question, then: How do we take up the challenge of preparing teachers to teach in socially just, equitable, and democratic ways? Part of the challenge is in how teacher knowledge and teacher learning has been conceptualized in national discourse. Cochran Smith (2000) has argued that at the heart of efforts to reframe teacher education in this new century is how we understand the "questions that matter." Narrow conceptions of the knowledge question and the learning question has framed teacher knowledge and teacher learner around how much a teacher knows, where development is conceived as a rote endeavor rather than a process of growth, development, and transformation. What is more she argues, outcomes, while taken up differentially by the research literature, the policy arena, and the media, contribute to the narrow conceptions of teachers and teaching by focusing on the relationship between teacher qualifications and training and student learning. Each of the constructions undermine efforts to build a just and democratic society for they view social justice as something that is taken up distinct from the regular work of teacher education (Cochran-Smith, 1999, 2001).

This text has drawn our attention to the ways in which youth experience science education in low-income urban communities. They present us with the struggles of teachers who work to make science education more equitable and empowering by working to live up to the democratic idea of a more just society. The chapters in the text have helped open up the discourse around democracy, social justice and science education. They have reminded us that the democratic ideal of social justice must be front and center of science education if it is to have a sustained impact on youth. The chapters show us how teaching ought to be framed as a political activity and learning as transformative. If issues of social justice are to be taken up in deep and consequential ways, then discourse on teacher learning and teacher knowledge must embrace how teachers' work is inherently "interpretive, political, theoretical, as well as practical, strategic, and local" and where teacher learning is viewed as an on-going "process of transformation" (Cochran Smith, 2000, p. 18). The chapters before remind us that the oppressive tendencies and regressive policies of society can be counteracted by viewing students from an anti-deficit perspective – as "makers of knowledge" who are capable of meeting rigorous, high expectations.

In building democratic science education, teachers need opportunities to develop conceptual tools that help them to view their classrooms, students, and practices differently. We have suggested that the tools of Voice, Authority, and Critical Science Literacy are important.

Upadhyay's chapters helps us to see how one teachers's ability to listen to her students' voices helped her to position students not only as authors of science, but authorities. Such authority in her classroom space was transformational because it helped students to leverage their cultural knowledge and experience towards building important skills in evidence-based reasoning and argumentation. As Upadhyay reminds us, classrooms are not neutral spaces. Culture and knowledge gained from experience are always a part of the frames that youth bring to learning new knowledge at school. As he suggests, one way to help students engage in science is to allow them to bring their knowledge from their own experience into the classroom.

The combination of science and home knowledge provides a better basis for the understanding of science content and concepts.

Likewise Seiler reveals how democratic science education emanates from the lives of the learners necessitates new forms of participation by teachers and students. The young teacher in her chapter was confronted with constraints of English as the language of instruction, lack of resources, effects of rurality (poverty, violence, and HIV/AIDS), and limited job prospects for his students. And yet, he created new patterns of science participation that were learner-initiated and centralized their voices in the process. Seiler reminds us of how situated democratic science education is. She states that "North American readers may see Msizi's classroom as falling short of participatory democracy in many ways" and yet, the practices in this space challenged and subverted the oppressive norms for the students and teacher there.

The youth in GET City (Chapter 4) displayed critical science literacy in their investigation of the carbon footprint of their canteen lunch to uncover how their free lunch was costly to them in environmental terms. To do so, the youth needed to be adept at expressing themselves in scientific terms so as to have useful tools and knowledges that will equip them to critically examine local issues relevant to mathematics and science. At the same time, they also needed to be able to articulate the concerns of their communities drawn from pertinent local issues in order to leverage on their acquired science content skills and knowledges. In so doing, the youth also engage with the complexities that often surround socio-scientific issues. This is an important learning outcome as the youth seriously consider multiple perspectives of an issue. As the youth uncovered the many environmentally un-friendly aspects of the club lunch, the youth crafted, socio-scientific critique jostles against the counter script of the school district providing a somewhat nutritionally balanced lunch daily, free of charge, to the children who attend the community club, many of whom come from low-income backgrounds. How are the youth and teachers at GET City to reconcile the two scripts, both of which are important and essential in different ways? Growing children need nutritionally balanced meals and the free lunch is a laudable social service that the school district is providing for the entire summer when students are out of schools (and so have no other access to free lunches). Yet, the manner in which the free lunches have been packaged and transported raised important concerns for the very youth benefitting from the lunch, since they will likely to be the ones reaping the environmental consequences of a high carbon footprint. Critical science literacy works to equip youth to grapple with such science-related tensions in their everyday lives with more knowledge and facility.

While these chapters offer the tools of Voice, Authority and Critical Science Literacy, they also help us to re-image how to attend to what is "inequitable" in urban science education. Often when equitable science education is discussed, the issue of resources, teacher pay, and course offers dominate the discourse. These are fundamental and should always be on the table. However, there are more layers to this debate that these chapters bring to the fore. Cutting across these chapters is an implicit focus on the problem spaces that frame the challenge of equity in science education today – problem spaces that can serve as both a challenge and place for transformation if teachers bring the tools of democratic education to them. Three of the spaces that cut across the chapters include: the goals and outcomes of education, the place of education, and science & society.

EXPANDING GOALS & OUTCOMES

As Rick Duschl (2008) recently argued: we have to move beyond conceptual goals to include epistemological and social goals as well in science education. This point calls attention to how learning science is as much about learning to participate in the cultural practices of science as it is about a knowledge base. Studies on equity and diversity, primarily from sociocultutal perspectives, unpack this further for us. Considerations of who one might be to succeed and the kinds of resources one might access and activate towards meaningful engagement is deeply embedded in cultural contexts. Cultural historical perspectives remind us that learning happens in both vertical (novice to expert) and horizontal (across communities) ways. Supporting youth in being able, for example, to translate ideas such as carbon cycling in culturally relevant ways for others across the communities they live, learn, and play should be *just as important* as being able to give a reasoned and abstracted explanation of such scientific ideas in the classroom. In chapter 4 (Alhoyokem et al.,) we see youth construct scientific documentaries that are at once critical of the current food system and respectful of the challenges faced in particular by low-income communities in eating in a sustainable way. Knowing the environmental impact of their carbon footprint was important to their narrative, but so was knowing how and why that footprint took shape in their communities. In chapter 3 (O'Neill) we see youth engaging in improvisation by leveraging science towards transforming how they learn science in schools and what teachers expect of them. The outcomes of education matter beyond standard content knowledge and practice, but standard content knowledge and practice are not marginal to these more critical outcomes of science education.

This last point about vertical and horizontal learning raises further consideration for how we recognize progress towards any learning goals in science education. That one can recognize oneself as a "make a difference expert" because of what they know and the actions they can take <u>because</u> of what they know *should not be distinct* from learning in schools. That one might leverage multimodal literacies or digital technologies to engage deeply in science and to communicate scientifically with others is also an equity issue that cuts with both sides of the sword – in terms of the range of representations of self and science made possible through these modalities but also in terms of who has access anyway.

THE PLACE OF LEARNING

Nel Noddings has written that standards education which can promote a more generic education from "anywhere" may easily deteriorate to an education from "nowhere." Can or should science education be localized in ways that incorporate rich new research findings of how sense of place shapes how and why students engage in science in their classrooms? I (Angie) recall a study we did with teachers who, working with the Cornell Ornithology Lab, implemented a place-base unit to teach taxonomy and environmental statistics – a tested topic in NY. By a range of accounts including student test scores, the unit, which focused on observing and analyzing neighborhood pigeons and pigeon counts, was highly successful. Students "got it". But in post unit interviews, we learned that students hadn't shifted at all in their fundamental views about pigeons – they were still rats with wings, their neighborhood has lots of them because it's a poor neighborhood, and why didn't they also study how to clean up their neighborhood to fix the pigeon problem? Should these have been incorporated in a unit on taxonomy? Perhaps, but more importantly, how we scaffold teachers through standards to think about how place – as a cultural, historical, geographical, and social space – matters. For those whose cultural knowledge and experiences sit outside the normative curriculum, these considerations matter the most. Attention to these spaces expands the question from inequality (sources and resources) –which is painfully important – to further include the role of culture and diversity in what and how opportunities for powerful science learning and practice are made (and how we recognize progress towards it), and also to the kind of just society we may try to foster through our work in science education.

Emdin in Chapter 7 highlights the importance of the place of learning when he carefully examines the dynamics and interactions between different groups of students in a city with a diverse and ever-increasing migrant population. The context of science learning in his urban science classroom was brought to bear in how he enacted the 3Cs to help foster solidarity amongst students while at the same time empowering them to collaboratively be authentic learners and inquirers of science. Seiler showed, in Chapter 6, how the young teacher Msizi were strategic in utilizing strategies that broke down the "wall of silence" most educators in South Africa accept as the norm for non-White students. Msizi, cognizant of the cultural, historical, political, geographical and social space of his students, enacted a pedagogy that encouraged his students to venture into unchartered ground – testing out scientific words in English, answering questions, and asking questions. These steps forward were made possible by Msizi's keen awareness of the local context of his students and his efforts to tailor his science instruction to the needs and concerns of his students.

SCIENCE AND SOCIETY

Indeed, learning about and practicing democratic science education is not distinct from learning about and practicing the discipline one teaches. Democratic education and in our case, teaching science, ought not be thought about separately. Science, as both a discipline of study and an everyday practice, is a particularly important domain for fostering equity and social justice across all sectors of society – core ideals of democratic practice. In today's increasingly technological and scientifically driven world, a sound science education offers access to high paying and powerful professions. It provides individuals with the knowledge and skills for critically understanding and evaluating their bodies, environments, communities and worlds. Unfortunately science literacy is often assumed by many to be constituted of mastery of content knowledge without consideration for how students learn to *use that knowledge within their own worlds*. Part of learning to teach a democratic science education is to recognize the ways in which being scientifically literate allows students to express voice and enact forms of authority within and across their own lives, communities and classrooms. Democratic science education seeks to equip all students with rigorous science knowledge and skills while at the same time empowering them with a sense of critical science agency that positions them as able learners and inquirers of science *now*, and who are capable of continued engagement with science in the future. Democratic science education also empowers students to fruitfully utilize their increasing science knowledge and expertise to better their lives and those of others in their communities. Jhumki's students, Neil and Donya, exemplify these ideals of democratic science education in their intensive efforts in researching science topics that interests them, allows them to take up new roles to help their peers, and open doors for career possibilities for both youths.

CONCLUSION

Jhumki started this book with a desire to document what democratic science education looks like, why it is important, what roles teachers and students can play in a democratic science classroom, and how democratic science teaching fosters a learning environment where all students, especially urban, low-income youth who are deemed most unlikely to succeed, can have access to rigorous science instruction where their voice, concerns, interests, strengths, and ideas are woven into the classroom science discourse. Jhumki's colleagues, the authors of these chapters, who share her vision for addressing inequalities in science education for marginalized students have come together to offer a set of images of what democratic science education can look like in various contexts. Through the different chapters, stories of teachers and students have been shared, each unique to its local context and particular concerns. These varied chapters showcase the different ways in which democratic science education can be enacted and supported. It is our hope that the stories in this book will serve as helpful examples of how democratic science education can create empowering classrooms in science across different learning environments, so that all students can indeed be bona fide beneficiaries of the much touted goal, "Science for All."

REFERENCES

Aikenhead, G. S. (1996). Science education: Border crossing into the subculture of science. *Studies in Science Education, 27*, 1–52.

Aikenhead, G. S., & Jegede, O. J. (1999). Cross-cultural science education: A cognitive explanation of a cultural phenomenon. *Journal of Research in Science Teaching, 36*, 269–287.

Aikenhead, G. S. (1997). Toward a first nations cross-cultural science and technology curriculum. *Science Education, 81*, 217–238.

Akatugba, A. H., & Wallace, J. (1999). Socio-cultural influences on physics students' use of proportional reasoning in a non-Western country. *Journal of Research in Science Teaching, 36*, 269–287.

Appiah, K. (2006). *Cosmopolitanism: Ethics in a world of strangers.* New York: W.W. Norton & Company, Inc.

Apple, M. W. (1993). *Official knowledge: Democratic education in a conservative age.* New York: Routledge.

Au, K. H. (1980). *Participation structures in a reading lesson with Hawaiian children: Analysis.*

Banks, J. (2008). Diversity, group identity, and citizenship education in a global age. *Educational Researcher, 37*(3), 129–139.

Basu, J. S., & Calabrese Barton, A. (2007). Developing a sustained interest in science among urban minority youth. *Journal of Research in Science Teaching, 44*(3), 466–489.

Benchmarks for Scientific Literacy. (2003). *Project 2061.* Cary, NC: Oxford University Press.

Benhabib (Ed.). *Democracy and difference: Contesting the boundaries of the political* (pp. 67–94), Princeton, NJ: Princeton University Press.

Benhabib, S. (1996). *Toward a deliberative model of democratic legitimacy.* In Seyla

Bennett, L., Collins, J., & Emdin, C. (2007). A metalogue on urban schools and science classrooms: Student voices on research products. *Cultural Studies of Science Education, 2*, 387–392.

Blackburn, M. (2004). Understanding agency beyond school-sanctioned activities. *Theory into Practice, 43*, 102–110.

Bohman, J. (1997). The public spheres of the world citizen. In J. Bohmanand & M. Lutz-Bachmann (Eds.), *Perpetual peace: Essays on Kant's cosmopolitan ideal* (pp. 179–200). MA: MIT Press.

Bouillion, L. M., & Gomez, L. M. (2001). Connecting school and community with science learning: Real world problems and school-community partnerships as contextual scaffold. *Journal of Research in Science Teaching, 38*(8), 878–898.

Brickhouse, N. (1994). Bringing in the outsiders: Reshaping the science of the future. *Journal of Curriculum Studies, 26*, 401–416.

Brickhouse, N., & Potter, J. (2001). Young women's scientific identity formation in an urban context. *Journal of Research in Science Teaching, 38*(8), 965–980.

Bridges, D. (1979). *Education, democracy and discussion.* Atlantic Highlands, NJ: Humanities Press.

Brown, B. (2006). It isn't no slang that can be said about this stuff: Language, identity, and appropriating science discourse. *Journal of Research in Science Teaching, 43*, 96–126.

Bryan, L., & Atwater, M. (2002) Teacher beliefs and cultural models: A challenge for scienceteacher preparation programs. *Science Education, 86*, 821–839.

Butler, J. (2004). *Undoing gender.* New York: Routledge.

Calabrese Barton, A. (1998). Examining the social and scientific roles of invention in science education. *Research in Science Education, 28*, 133–151.

Calabrese Barton, A. (1998a). Reframing "science for all" through the politics of poverty. *Educational Policy, 12*(5), 5–541.

Calabrese Barton, A. (1998b). Teaching science with homeless children: Pedagogy, representation, and identity. *Journal of Research in Science Teaching, 35*, 379–394.

Calabrese Barton, A. (2001). Science education in urban settings: seeking new ways of praxis through critical ethnography. *Journal of Research in Science Teaching, 38*, 899–917.

REFERENCES

Cazden, C. B. (1988). *Classroom discourse: The language of teaching and learning*. Portsmouth, New Hampshire: Heinemann Educational Books, Inc.

Cazden, C. B. (2001). *Classroom discourse: The language of teaching and learning* (2nd ed.). Portsmouth, NH: Heinemann.

Chambers, S. (2003). Deliberative democratic theory. *Annual Review of Political Science, 6*, 307–332.

Clark, J., & Linder, C. (2006). *Changing teaching, changing times: Lessons from a South African Township science classroom*. Rotterdam: Sense Publishers.

Cochran-Smith, M. (1995). Color blindness and basket making are not the answers: Confronting the dilemmas of race, culture, and language diversity in teacher education. *American Educational Research Journal, 32*, 493–522.

Cochran-Smith, M. (1999). Learning to teach for social justice. In G. A. Griffin (Ed.), *The education of teachers* (pp. 114–144). Chicago: University of Chicago Press.

Cochran-Smith, M. (2000). The future of teacher education: Framing the questions that matter. *Teaching Education, 11*(1), 13–24.

Cochran-Smith, M. (2001). Higher standards for prospective teachers: What's missing from the discourse? *Journal of Teacher Education, 52*(3), 179–181.

Cochran-Smith, M. (2004). Walking the road: Race, diversity, and social justice in.

Committee on Trends in Federal Spending on Scientific and Engineering Research, National Research Council. (2001). *Trends in federal support of research and graduate education*. Washington, DC.

Department of Education, Republic of South Africa. (2003). *National curriculum statement, grades 10–12, physical sciences*. Pretoria: Government Printer.

Deutsch, M. (2006). A framework for thinking about oppression and change. *Social Justice Research, 19*(1).

Dewey, J. (1933). *How we Think: A restatement of the relation of reflective thinking to the educative process (1910)* (Rev. ed.). Boston: Heath.

Diamondidis, E. (1998). A language sensitive science teacher training approach. *English Teaching Forum, 36*, 39–43.

Dillon, J. T. (1994). *Deliberation in education and society*. Norwood, NJ: Ablex.

Elmesky, R., & Tobin, K. (2005). Expanding our understanding of urban science education by expanding the roles of students as researchers. *Journal of Research in Science Teaching, 42*, 807–828.

Emdin, C. (2007). Exploring the contexts of urban science classrooms: Investigating corporate and communal practices. *Cultural Studies of Science Education, 2*, 319–350.

Emdin, C. (In press). Affiliation and alienation: Hip-hop, rap, and urban science education. *Journal of Curriculum Studies*.

Fishkin, J. S., & Luskin, R. C. (2005). Experimenting with a democratic ideal: Deliberative polling and public opinion. *Acta Politica, 40*, 284–298.

Fiske, J. (1989). *Reading the popular*. Boston: Unwin Hyman.

Foucault, M. (1977). *Discipline and Punish*. New York: Pantheon.

Foucault, M. (1982). The subject and power. *Critical Inquiry, 8*, 777–795.

Freire, P. (1970). *Pedagogy of the oppressed*. New York: Continuum.

Freire, P. (1998). *Teachers as cultural workers: Letters to those who dare to teach*. Boulder, CO: Westview Press.

Fung, A. (2004). *Empowered participation*. Princeton, NJ: Princeton University Press.

Furman, M., & Calabrese Barton, A. (2006). Capturing urban student voices in the creation of a science mini-documentary. *Journal of Research in Science Teaching, 3*(7), 667–694.

Gee, J. (1999). *An introduction to discourse analysis. Theory and method*. London:Routledge.

Gollub, J., & Spital, R. (2002). Advanced physics in high schools. *Physics Today, 55*, 48–53.

Gonçalves e Silva, P. B. (2004). Citizenship education in Brazil: The contributions of Indian peoples and blacks in the struggle for citizenship. In J. A. Banks (Ed.), *Diversity and citizenship education: Global perspectives* (pp. 185–217). San Francisco: Jossey-Bass.

Goodin, R. E. (2005). Sequencing deliberative moments. *Acta Politica, 40*, 182–196.

Goodlad, J. I. (1990). *Teachers for our nations' schools*. San Francisco: Jossey-Bass.

Goodman, D. (2001). *Promoting diversity and social justice: Educating people from privileged*.

Grant, C. (1994). Best practices in teacher education for urban schools: Lessons from the multicultural teacher education literature. *Action in Teacher Education, 16*(3), 2–18.

Grant, C. A., & Secada, W. G. (1990). Preparing teachers for diversity. In W. R. Houston (Ed.), *Handbook of research on teacher education* (pp. 404–422). New York: MacMillan.

Grant, K. E., O'Koon, J. H., Davis, T. H., Roache, N. A., Poindexter, L. M., Armstrong, M. L., et al. (2000). Protective factors affecting low-income urban African American youth exposed to stress. *Journal of Early Adolescence, 20*, 388–418.

Greeno, J., & Goldman, S. (Eds.), (1998). *Thinking practices in mathematics and science learning.* Mahwah, NJ: Lawrence Erlbaum Associates.

Grimshaw, A. D. (1982). Sound image data records for research on social interaction. *Sociological Methods and Research, 11*(2), 121–144.

groups. Thousand Oaks, CA: Sage.

Gutierrez, K., & Rogoff, B. (2003). Cultural ways of learning: Individual traits or repertoires of practice. *Educational Researcher, 32*, 19–25.

Gutmann, A. (2004). Unity and diversity in democratic multicultural education: Creative and destructive tensions. In J. A. Banks (Ed.), *Diversity and citizenship education: Global perspectives* (pp. 71–96). San Francisco: Jossey-Bass.

Gutmann, A., & Thompson, D. (1996). *Democracy and disagreement.* Cambridge, MA: Harvard University Press.

Gutmann, A., & Thompson, D. (2004). *Why deliberative democracy?* Princeton, NJ: Princeton University Press.

Habermas, J. (1996). 1996a. *Between facts and norms. Contributions to a discourse theory of law and, the democracy.* Cambridge, MA: MIT Press.

Habermas, J. (2005). Concluding comments on empirical approaches to deliberative politics. *Acta Politica, 40*, 384–392.

Hammond, & Sykes, G. (Eds.), *Teaching as the learning profession: Handbook of policy and practice* (pp. 33–53). San Francisco: Jossey Bass.

Harding, S. (1993). Rethinking standpoint epistemology: What is "strong objectivity"? In L. Alcoff & E. Potter (Eds.), *Feminist Epistemologies* (pp. 49–82). London: Routledge.

Heble, A. (2005). Improvising matters: Rights, risks and responsibilities. *Critical Studies in Improvisation/ Études critiques en improvisation, 1*(2), 1–3.

Hobson, A. (2003). Physics literacy, energy and the environment. *Physics Education, 38*, 109–114.

Hofmeyer, J., & Buckland, P. (1992). Education system change in South Africa. In R. McGregor & A. McGregor (Eds.), *McGregor's alternatives.* Kenwyn: Juta's & Co.

Holland, D., Lachicotte, W., Jr., Skinner, D., & Cain, C. (1998). *Identity and agency in cultural worlds.* Cambridge, MA: Harvard University Press.

Holland, D. (1998). *Identity and agency in cultural worlds.* Cambridge: Harvard University Press.

Howie, S., & Scherman, V. (2008). The achievement gap between science classrooms and historic inequalities. *Studies in Educational Evaluation, 34*, 118–130.

Ingersoll, R., & Perda, D. (2010). Is the supply of mathematics and science teachers sufficient? *American Educational Research Journal.*

Ingersoll, R. M. (2003). Is there a shortage among mathematics and science teachers? *Science Educator, 12*, 1–9.

Jansen, J. (1998). Curriculum reform in South Africa: A critical analysis of outcomes-based education. *Cambridge Journal of Education, 28*, 321–331.

Jenkins, E. (2006). The student voice and school science education. *Studies in Science Education, 42*, 49–88.

Kao, G., & Thompson, J. S. (2003). Racial and ethnic stratification in educational achievement and attainment. *Annual Review of Sociology, 29*, 417–442.

Kelly, A. (2004). *Newton in the big apple: Issues of equity in physics access and enrollment in New York City public schools.* Paper presented at the American Association of Research Education, San Diego, CA.

REFERENCES

Kenny, M. E., Sparks, E., & Jackson, J. (2007). Striving for social justice. In E. Aldarondo (Ed.), *Advancing social justice through clinical practice*. London: Routledge.

Kharsany, A., Carrara, H., Frohlich, J., Abdool Karim, S. S., & Abdool Karim, Q. (2005, June). *HIV seroprevalence in rural KwaZulu Natal in 2004 - Implications for research and programmatic priority setting*. Paper presented at the 2nd South Africa AIDS Conference in Durban, South Africa.

Kincheloe, J., & Steinberg, S. (1998). *Students as researchers: Creating classrooms that matter*. New York: Routledge.

Kress, G., Jewitt, C., & Ogborn, J. (2001). *Multimodal teaching and learning: The rhetorics of the science classroom*. London and New York: Continuum International.

Ladson-Billings, G. (1999a). Preparing teachers for diverse student populations: A critical race perspective. In A. Iran-Nejad & C. D. Pearson (Eds.), *Review of research in education* (Vol. 24, pp. 211–248). Washington, DC: American Educational Research Association.

Ladson-Billings, G. (1999b). Preparing teachers for diversity: Historical perspectives, current trends, and future directions. In L. Darling-Hammond & G. Sykes (Eds.), *Teaching as the learning profession: Handbook of policy and practice* (pp. 86–123). San Francisco: Jossey-Bass.

Ladson-Billings, G., & Tate, W. F. (1995). *Toward a critical race theory of education*.

Lampert, M., & Ball, D. (1998). *Teaching, multimedia, and mathematics: Investigations of real practice*. New York: Teachers College Press.

Lampert, M., & Ball, D. (1999). Aligning teacher education with contemporary K-12 reform visions. In L. Darling-

Lane, J., & Ersson, S. (2003). *Democracy: A comparative approach*. New York: Routledge.

Laugksch, R. (2000). Scientific literacy: A conceptual overview. *Science Education, 84*, 71–94.

LaVan, S., & Beers, J., (2005). The role of cogenerative dialogue in learning to teach and transforming learning environments. In K. Tobin, R. Elmesky & G. Seiler (Eds.), *Improving urban science education: New roles for teachers, students and researchers* (pp. 147–164). New York: Rowman and Littlefield.

Lave, J., & Wenger, E. (1991). *Situated learning: Legitimate peripheral participation*. Cambridge: Cambridge University Press.

Lee, O. (2001). Culture and language in science education: What do we know and what do we need to know. *Journal for Research in Science Teaching, 38*(5), 499–501.

Lee, O. (2002). Science inquiry for elementary students from diverse backgrounds. In W.G.

LeGrange, L. (2007). Integrating Western and indigenous knowledge systems: The basis for effective science education in South Africa? *International Review of Education, 53*, 577–591.

Lemke, J. (1990). *Talking science: Language, learning and values*. Norwood, NJ: Ablex.

Lemke, J. L. (2000). Articulating communities: Sociocultural perspectives on science education. *Journal of research in Science Teaching, 38*(3), 296–316.

Lipka, J. (1998). *Transforming the culture of schools: Yup'ik Eskimo examples*. Mahwah, NJ: Erlbaum.

Lipman, P. (2004). *High stakes education: inequity, globalization and urban school reform*. New York: Routledge/Falmer.

Marshall, T. H. (1964). *Class citizenship and social development. Essays of T.H Marshall*. Westport, Greenwood.

Martin, J. (2008). Pedagogy of the alienated: Can Freirean teaching reach working-class students? *Equity and Excellence in Education, 41*, 31–44.

McDonald, M. (2005). The integration of social justice into teacher education programs. *Journal of Teacher Education, 56*(5), 418–435.

McMahon, B., & Portelli, J. P. (2004). Engagement for what? Beyond popular discourses of student engagement. *Leadership and Policy in Schools, 3*, 59–76.

Michaels, S., O'Connor, C., & Resnick, L. B. (2008). Deliberative discourse idealized and realized: Accountable talk in the classroom and in civic life. *Studies in Philosophy and Education, 27*, 283–297.

Miller, J (2002). Civic scientific literacy: A necessity in the 21st century. *Federation of American Scientists Public Interest Report, 55*, 3–6.

Moje, E. B., Ciechanowski, K. M., Kramer, K., Ellis, L., Carrillo, R., Collazo, T., et al. (2004). Working toward third space in content area literacy: An examination of everyday funds of knowledge and discourse. *Reading Research Quarterly, 39*(1), 38–70.

Moll, L. C., Amanti, C., Neff, D., & Gonzalez, N. (1992). Funds of knowledge for teaching: Using a qualitative approach to connect homes and classrooms. *Theory into Practice, 31*, 132–141.

Moreno-Lopez, I. (2005, Fall). Sharing power with students: The critical language classroom. *Radical Pedagogy, 7*. Retrieved from http://radicalpedagogy.icaap.org/content/issue7_2/

Mulvey, P., & Nicholson, S. (2003). Enrollment and degree report. *American Institute of Physics.*

Murrell, P. (2006). Toward social justice in urban education. *Equity & Excellence in Education, 39*(1), 81–90.

Murrell, P. C. (2002). *African-centered pedagogy: Developing schools of achievement for African American children.* Albany, NY: State University of New York Press.

Mutz, D. C. (2006). *Hearing the other side: Deliberative versus participatory democracy.* New York: Cambridge University Press

Nanz, P., & Jens, S. (2005). Assessing the democratic quality of deliberation in international governance - criteria and research strategies. *Acta Politica, 40*, 368–383.

National Research Council. (1996). *National science education standards.* Washington, DC: National Academy Press.

National Science Foundation, Division of Science Resources Statistics. (2007). *Women, minorities, and persons with disabilities in science and engineering: 2007*, NSF 07-315. Arlington, VA. Available from http://www.nsf.gov/statistics/wmpd

National, Science Board. (2000). *Science and engineering indicators–2000.* Arlington, VA: National Science Foundation.

Nelson Mandela Foundation. (2005). Emerging voices: A report on education in South African rural communities. Capetown, South Africa: NSRC Press.

Nespor, J. (1997). *Tangled up in school: Politics, space, bodies, and signs in the educational process.* Mahwah, NJ: Lawrence Erlbaum Associates.

New York City Department of Education. (2004). *School information* [online]. Available: http://www.nycenet.edu

Noddings, N. (1992) *The challenge to care in schools: An alternative approach to education.* New York: Teachers College Press.

O'Donoghue, J., Kirshner, B., & McLaughlin, M. (2002). Introduction: Moving youth participation forward. *New Directions for Youth Development,* (96), 5–7.

Oakes, J. (1985). *Keeping track: How schools structure inequality.* New Haven, CT: Yale University Press.

Oakes, J. (2000). *Course-taking and achievement: Inequalities that endure and change.* A keynote paper presented at the National Institute for Science Education Forum, Detroit, MI.

Oakes, J. (2005). *Keeping track: How schools structure inequality.* New Haven, CT: Yale University Press of a culturally appropriate instructional event. *Anthropology and Education Quarterly, 11*(2), 91–115.

Oulton, C., Dillon, J., & Grace, M. (2004). Reconceptualizing the teaching of controversial issues. *International Journal of Science Education, 26*, 411–423.

Pace, J., & Hemmings, A. (2006). *Classroom authority: Theory, research, and practice.* Mahwah, NJ: Lawrence Erlbaum Associates, Inc.

Parker, W. C. (2003). *Teaching democracy: Unity and diversity in public life.* New York: Teachers College Press.

Parsons, E. C. (2003). Culturalizing instruction: Creating a more inclusive context for learning for African American students. *The High School Journal, 86*(4), 23–30.

Portelli, L., & Solomon, R. (Eds.), (2001). *The erosion of democracy in education: From critique to possibilities.* Calgary: Detselig Enterprises.

Probyn, M. (2006). Language and learning science in South Africa. *Language and Education, 20*(5), 391–414.

REFERENCES

PROVIDE. (2005). *A profile of KwaZulu-Natal: Demographics, poverty, inequality and unemployment.* PROVIDE Technical Paper Series (Vol. 2). Elsenburg, South Africa: PROVIDE Project. Available online at www.elsenburg.com/provide

Rahm, J. (2001). Emergent learning opportunities in an Inner-City youth gardening program. *Journal of Research in Science Teaching, 39*(2), 164–184.

Rawls, J. (1971). *A theory of justice.* Cambridge, MA: The Belknap Press of Harvard University Press.

Roth, W.-M., Tobin, K., & Zimmerman, A. (2002). Coteaching/cogenerative dialoguing: learning environments research as classroom praxis. *Learning Environments Research, 5.* 1–28.

Reinhiller, N. (1996). Coteaching: New variations on a not-so-new practice. *Teacher Education and Special Education, 19*(1), 34–48.

Roderick, M., & Engle, M. (2001). The grasshopper and the ant: Motivational responses of low-achieving students to high-stakes testing. *Educational Evaluation and Policy Analysis, 23*(3), 197–227.

Roth, W. M., Tobin, K., & Zimmerman, A. (2002). Coteaching/cogenerative dialoguing: Learning environments research as classroom praxis. *Learning Environments Research, 5,* 1–28.

Roth, W. M., & Calabrese Barton, A. (2004). *Rethinking science literacy.* New York: RoutledgeFalmer.

Sanders, L. (1997). Against deliberation. *Political Theory, 3,* 347–376.

Satz, D. (2007). Equality, adequacy, and education for citizenship. *Ethics, 117,* 623–648.

Secada (Ed.), *Review of research in education* (Vol. 26, pp. 23–69). Washington, DC: American Educational Research Association.

Seiler, G. (2001). Reversing the "standard" direction: Science emerging from the lives of African American students. *Journal of Research in Science Teaching, 38,* 1000–1014.

Seiler, G., & Gonsalves, A. (In press). Student-powered science: Science education for and by African American students. *Equity and Excellence in Education.*

Sharma, A. (2007). Making (electrical) connections: Exploring student agency in a school in India. *Science Education,* 1–23.

Sharma, A. (in press). Science teacher as a bricoleur. *Cultural Studies of Science Education.*

Shumba, O. (1999). Relationship between secondary science teachers' orientation to traditional culture and beliefs concerning science instructional ideology. *Journal of Research in Science Teaching, 36,* 333–355.

Smith, M. C. (2004). *Walking the road.* New York: Teachers College press.

Smitherman, G. (1977). *Talkin and testifyin: The language of Black America.* Detroit, MI: Wayne State University Press.

Sokoloff, D. R., & Thornton, R. K. (1997). Using interactive lecture demonstrations to create an active learning environment. *Physics Teacher, 35,* 340–347.

Speight, S. L. (2000). *Multiculturalism and the status quo.* Paper presented at the annual Teachers College Winter Roundtable on Cross-Cultural Psychology and Education, New York.

Strauss, A., & Corbin, J. (1998). *Basics of qualitative research: grounded theory procedures and techniques.* Sage Publishers.

Tan, E., & Barton, A. (2007). From peripheral to central, the story of Melanie's metamorphosis in an urban middle school science class. *Science Education,* 1–24.

teacher education. New York: Teachers College Press.

Teachers College Record, 97, 47–68.

Tobin, K., Elmesky, R., & Seiler, G. (Eds.), (2005). *Improving urban science education: New roles for teachers, students and researchers.* New York: Rowman & Littlefield.

Turner, E., & Font, B. (2003). *Fostering critical mathematical agency: urban middle school students engage in mathematics to understand, critique and act upon their world.* Paper presented at the American Education Studies Association Conference, Mexico City.

U.S Constitution, XIV Amendment. Section 1.

United Nations General Assembly. (1948). *Universal declaration of human rights.* http://www.un.org/Overview/rights.html

Upadhyay, B. (2006). Using students' lived experiences in an urban science classroom: An elementary school teacher's thinking. *Science Education, 90,* 94–110.

Van Heuvelen, A. (1991). Learning to think like a physicist: A review of research based instructional strategies. *American Journal of Physics, 59*, 891–897.

Walzer, M. (1983). *Spheres of justice: A defense of pluralism and equality.* New York: Basic Books.

Wiedeman, C. R. (2002). Teacher preparation, social justice, equity: A review of the literature. *Equity & Excellence in Education, 35*(3), 200–211.

Williams, D. R. (1999). Race, socioeconomic status, and health: The added effects of racism and discrimination. *Annals of the New York Academy of Sciences, 896*, 173–88.

Yin, R. (1993). *Applications of Case Study Research.* Sage Publishers.

Yin, R. (1994). *Case study research: design and methods.* Thousand Oaks, CA: Sage Publications.

Young, I. M. (2001). Activist challenges to deliberative democracy. *Political Theory, 29*: 670–690.

Young, I. M. (1990). *Justice and the politics of difference.* Princeton, NJ: Princeton University Press.

CPSIA information can be obtained at www.ICGtesting.com
Printed in the USA
BVOW030506250112

281328BV00004B/12/P